TO:
Deanna

The love of my life..!!
So much better together..!

[signature] 2019

To Be or Not To Be An Entrepreneur

by Steven H. Brown

Copyright © 2003 by Steven H. Brown

ISBN 0-7414-1598-4

Published by:

PUBLISHING.COM

519 West Lancaster Avenue
Haverford, PA 19041-1413
Info@buybooksontheweb.com
www.buybooksontheweb.com
Toll-free (877) BUY BOOK
Local Phone (610) 520-2500
Fax (610) 519-0261

Printed in the United States of America

Printed on Recycled Paper

Published August 2003

Contents

Foreword

First, this is not a how-to book. Although I have turned my dreams into a highly successful entrepreneurial business I don't have the secret to your success. Only you hold that key. Second, that being said, this book may be the most important tool you will find to help you determine whether you're cut out to be an entrepreneur. Notice I didn't say "if you have what it takes." Technically, I have what it takes to play pro baseball, wait tables, work in an office or do any number of other things able-bodied people do. But I'm not cut out to do any of those things. I'm an entrepreneur – it's what I do and it's who I am.

I was already married with a small daughter and a big mortgage when I decided to answer my own "to be or not to be an entrepreneur" question. I was also – for all intents and purposes – the sole support of my family. True, I had saved a bit over the years, having spent more than a decade in the corporate world. But was it really worth risking all of that – let alone, my future and theirs – on my dream?

If you answered "no" to that question I have already done you and your family a great service. You may not set the world on fire, but you won't lose your house, either.

Now let me tell you why I answered "yes" to that question: I believed in myself, and – as importantly – my family believed in me. My inner fire, combined with their trust in my abilities, kept me going during those early times when I wasn't even sure where I was going. For that, I am ever grateful to my wife, Marsha and daughter, Christina. I'm not sure what I can ever do to repay them but I'm sure they will continue to have a few ideas on the subject!

Today, shbrown.com is a thriving, growing and debt-free business. The year after 9/11 we doubled in size, and it doesn't look like we're going to stop anytime soon. Over the next one-hundred sixty-plus pages I'll share with you what I went through to get to where I am today, eleven years after I began my journey. And I won't sugar-coat a word of it.

If you picked up this book, you're probably at the fork in the road of your career. My goal is to simply help you get a better idea of which path is right for you. I know my answer. It's time for you to discover yours.

Introduction

"This job sucks, my boss is a jerk and if I have to tolerate just one more day of this crap I'm outta here!" Sound remotely familiar? I'm really not sure if these were the exact words I used on that fateful decision day in 1990, but they are close. I also remember hearing, "hey, the company thinks you're great and you are at the top of the pay scale. Hang in there and we will see what we can do for you." This was accompanied by a smile and a look that could be construed as either smirking and "you're totally screwed," or reassuring and "you're golden." You pick.

The rush hour drive home sent me into an introspective daze. It seemed clear that I had only two genuine alternatives, find a new job or venture off on my own. At this point, the latter was vastly more appealing. I mean what the hell, how much more impossible could starting my own company be as opposed to tolerating this garbage. No bosses manipulating my career. No office managers telling me what I can't order or timing my every movement. No butt kissing to stay one step ahead of the company rival. Instead I could be "large and in charge."

As the garage door opened to greet me, the idea of starting my own company hooked me like a tuna. Fortunately, the reality of what I was contemplating also delivered a right-cross to the chin and the rest of the evening was spent doing a reality check on my sanity. Who was I kidding? I had a child on the way, a mortgage payment you couldn't lift with a fork lift, no "pocket client" and no business plan. Yet, somehow I knew it was time to change.

In every office building and store front, in countless cubicles, apartments and homes, there are people who dream of starting their own business. I know, because I was one of them. Yet, this group is divided into two parts; those who do and those who do not. The decision to embark on the entrepreneurial journey is a heart-wrenching one at best and should not be taken lightly. I once had a fellow say to me, "thank goodness God made you ignorant, because if you knew how hard it was going to be to start your own company no one would do it." The reality is, truer words have never been spoken.

Still, there are many highly personal reasons for breaking away. In the best case, they will be so deeply ingrained that they will form the foundation of your personal resolve when the need arises – and it will. In the worst case situation, you will be naively overreacting to a sophomoric whim. Under this premise you are destined to fail. In either case, however, I would encourage you to get prepared for the challenge of your life.

But, "before you bolt," listen up.

I'll bet I've read a hundred books on the subject of entrepreneurialism. It's simply in my nature. Perhaps I take things too seriously. But this was going to be my one big shot. I didn't want to make mistakes that could have been easily avoided if only I had "done my homework."

The concept of homework really brings up the main pretense of this book and that is "preparation." If you grew up in the same system I did, namely the "programming" of the public schools, learning "right from wrong" from your hard working, middle-class parents, and the subtle "normalization" process of friends, job, spouse, children and patterns, then what you will read in this book may shock you, offend you, or – hopefully – inspire you and stimulate massive introspection. This is a critical step for those who feel a change in their lives is absolutely necessary, as I did.

There are literally hundreds of texts on the "how to's" of starting your own company. This book is all about learning to deal with yourself as you begin to embark on the entrepreneurial journey. To be sure, when you make the conscious decision to "stray from the norm," you will be greeted with a whole new set of experiences that, if taken in the right frame of mind, may prove more useful to you as a person than in the particular business you choose to enter.

This book could have been subtitled, "personal growth through adversity." If you're like me, you may have read a few books by – or seen speakers like – former POWs, tragedy victims, political figures, etc. But if you will be truthful with yourself, the real reason you sought them out in the first place was to compare and contrast yourself to people who had successfully met significant challenges in life. Personally, I was looking for qualities, attributes, personalities, quirks, and so on, that perhaps they had that I didn't. Flippantly, I wanted to learn about "the right stuff."

Before I started my company, masked under the veil of "pre-testing research," I went to visit a friend who was what I considered to be "successful." For the entire weekend, I watched for some "magic" that I was conspicuously lacking. On the plane home, I took copious notes on conversations, advice, philosophy, attitudes and personality characteristics. And you know what? The whole weekend came down to one statement, made in a trivial moment of openness. Pure and unanalyzed, he said, "I guess people like us were born to chase the horizon."

The truth of this statement cut me like an emotional laser. As I began to think back on my life, it became obvious that those things that I had decided to do, not those dictated by others, were the only ones that got accomplished...well. It boiled down to the difference between internal and external motivation. Ironically, for me, once a goal had been accomplished, it quickly became irrelevant. Clinically, I guess I'm a "means" person, with the "end" being only a small step away, expanding the view.

The chapters of this book are arranged in sequential order based on my experiences. The first four are about the process of making the decision to strike out on my own. I'll bet many of you reading this are at this stage. The remaining chapters deal with the "emotional rollercoaster" that followed. I did not write this book to be a "how to" guide. Rather, it was a way of better understanding my own challenges at the time, as well as providing guidance for those who would take on the challenge themselves. Many potentially great entrepreneurs of the future won't take action because they fear nothing more than the unknown. In this, there is no shame. But life is not a "dress rehearsal." It's the real thing, the "big show." Learning to deal with fear lubricates the gears of success, but you still have to turn the wheels.

Chapter 1

The Gerbil Wheel

"Life is what happens while you are making other plans."

– John Lennon

One Saturday morning, in the dead of a Midwestern winter, my wife and I were in a pet store in a local shopping mall. Having two German shepherds, the purchase of yet another animal, of any kind, was definitely out of the question. The store was arranged like hundreds of others. Dogs in one part. Birds in another. And, fish in still another. Aimless wandering led me to a corner of the shop that had one of those connecting tunnel systems for gerbils. I remember being quite impressed by its maze-like complexity and the way the gerbils seemed to enjoy chasing each other through the tubes.

At the bottom of the network was a small open area that had one of those exercise wheels. As I crouched to get a better look, I saw one particular gerbil running on the wheel. It interested me because it genuinely looked like this animal was enjoying the exercise, at first. However, as it got tired, things began to go awry. Once, it got going too fast and stumbled. The force of the wheel kept it in motion. The gerbil, clinging to the floor of the wheel, was flipped over on its back and crashed down on the other side. But it managed to get going again.

The construction of the wheel also interested me. Because of its tripod type support system, it was very stable. No matter how fast the gerbil ran, it would not tip over. The downside for the gerbil, though, was the fact that as long as the wheel was in motion, it was virtually impossible for it to

1

get off. It was only when the gerbil had completely given up and stopped running that the exit became accessible.

As I stood there and watched, with each revolution of the wheel the "gears" in my head began to turn as well. A growing anguish came over me and I remember thinking that my whole life seemed to be symbolically played out in the corner of a mall pet store. For not unlike the gerbil, I was starting to realize that in a circle, beginnings and ends can become blurred. And, sooner or later, you come to grips with the fact that you are on a "marathon to nowhere." If that weren't bad enough, in the corporate race, someone else controls the pace. You are running simply to survive.

Over the course of the next several months, I became very introspective and moody. This was in direct opposition to my core personality. I was simply "out of balance" with myself. Oriental religious philosophy speaks a great deal about "balance" and "internal harmony." A "oneness" of sorts. But at a point in my life where I felt the crushing weight of an imposed "under thumb" structure, "getting through it" on a daily basis far outweighed the tiny counterbalance at the other end. This was not a feeling of "oneness" with my environment; this was being in service of it. Was I the only one who was confronting this challenge?

With my awareness raised, I began to watch the actions of others back at the office, looking for clues to my own dilemma. I happened to be having coffee one day with a lady who had one of those large wall calendars in her office. You know, the seasonal kind with snow and leaves and pumpkins and stuff. As we chatted about nothing in particular, I kept being drawn to something about this calendar. Then it struck me. With no less than draftsman-like precision, each passing day had been crossed off with a large "X" that stretched from corner to corner. I had to ask her why she did that. "It counts down the days till my vacation," she said with a struggling smile. How completely fatalistic this seemed to me. It was almost like, if she could go to sleep and wake up on the day of her vacation, life would be great. If memory serves me right, she got three weeks' vacation that year. According to my calculator, only 5.8% of her life was going to be great.

I'll bet everyone has a friend who is what I'll call "the master planner." This is the person who has truly made an art form out of combining vacation and company-paid holidays to maximize the time spent away from the office. You know this person. For hours, maybe days, they would work out various combinations to "stretch" each minute off. Generally, this was also the same person who wore out the phrase, "overworked and underpaid." "By God, they (the company) owe it to me, I have it coming and I'm takin' it." This person usually left at five and had the attention span of a three-year-old. Note: this guy managed to stretch his three weeks into five. I show 9.6% "greatness," or an increase of 65%. Heck of a deal!

The imbalance in my life had tangible, physical symptoms. Fatigue and withdrawal were the first. In junior high school, I played on a football team that went undefeated for three consecutive years. That same group of kids went on to three undefeated years in high school and a State Championship. For this team, winning was an institution. The thought of losing was simply unacceptable. Practicing was tough, but a joy. No one ever missed a practice except for severe injury, of which there were few. I remember the sense of beaming pride in wearing our jerseys to the school dance on Friday nights. This was a group that was supportive and each person gave 100%, because to do less was to damage the "team" as a whole. It was the best of times.

The same was not true, however, for the baseball team. We routinely got beat. Same group of kids, different situation and dramatically different results. Half the team had a "nagging" injury. Practice was a pain in the butt. Often, the coach, who was really an English teacher that needed the

3

money, had a "sub." Arguing among players, even during the game, was a common occurrence. These were the worst of times.

What does all this have to do with fatigue? Somehow, I felt the company "team" had lost its winning tradition. Or at least I no longer agreed with their definition of "winning." And not unlike the baseball team, I felt too tired to practice as hard as I should have. Interest in general was waning. Arguing between managers became commonplace, even during meetings. Worse yet, there was no talking at all. Objectives and motives began to diverge. And soon, I found myself not only not wearing the jersey, I stopped attending the dances.

I have to smile every time I think about a phrase I once heard, "subordinate wisdom." How many times have you said or heard someone say, "How can management be so blind, so stupid?" I freely admit to saying so at least 200 times, usually in the car on the way home. Clearly, it is not that people don't see things. It boils down to a question of what they choose to deal with. Remember, a certain degree of chaos and confusion is healthy. Also, from a different perspective, you might not define a situation as a "problem" that needs to be "fixed." A high-ranking executive at my old company once said to me, "Companies, by necessity, promote and enforce conformity. They are resistant to, and slow to act upon, change." Maybe I got tired of waiting.

One of the biggest resolves for me in this period was what I call the "end of the quest to be king." O.K. Assume for a minute you're overreacting. You're in a dues-paying timeframe. Things are tough. Maybe you just need to get away. But, what happens when you get to the point where you question your own goals? Let's face it. For many people in a company there is only one goal: get promoted, be the boss.

4

That is the competitive nature of the planet. But, what if you begin to seriously question whether or not you really want to "end up" like your boss? Or anyone in management, for that matter. They all seem so tired and bitter. Or quiet and political. Imagine getting promoted as being more "aggravation" than "elation." Maybe I not only stopped grabbing for the brass ring, I stopped wanting it.

Recently, I had the pleasure of meeting with a man who was at the Director level of General Motors. It was the first time I had been in his office. There, perched on his credenza, was an actual gerbil wheel. "Nice wheel," I said. "Personal joke," he replied. We both smiled.

Lesson #1

No matter what happens in your personal or professional life, it is important that you learn to find some form of joy in the journey, or the degree of difficulty will surely destroy your will to continue over time.

Chapter Two

Seminar Syndrome

"You may already be a loser."

– Form letter received by Rodney Dangerfield

I had never ordered anything off television, until now. Perhaps it's because I hate, really hate, being ripped off. Not just physically, but emotionally. Good intentions twisted to feelings of incompetence and gullibility nag at me for weeks. Somehow I just can't shake it. Generically, through a combination of increased competition and more savvy consumers, things are getting better. As long as you are willing to live with the old adage, "You get what you pay for," you'll be alright.

As a marketing professional, I can appreciate great sales pitches to the right audience. Talk about your perfect marketing targets – people who are truly looking for change in their lives, spiced with a sense of urgency, "ripe" for promoters of the "you too can be a millionaire" seminars and the like. Please don't misread my tonality here. There are some very good companies doing excellent work in this area. Believe me, I am the number-one advocate of self-improvement. I guess the tactics bug me. You've seen them. Beautiful Hawaiian settings for the shows, crashing waves, lovely ladies, the works. The promise is that "if you study the course, in a few short weeks, you'll be on the road to a better life."

This is the desired result, of course, for people who are in a slight state of depression at the time they receive the message. How many hundreds of thousands of people do you think that is? "Many," would be my guess.

7

I had the occasion to be flipping through the cable channels late one evening when I came across a program for a real estate seminar on cassette tapes. Real estate is one of the few ventures in my life where I had ever made any real money, so far. My father has been in "real estate of sorts" his whole life. So, on the whole, the subject interested me. As I watched a very "credible" looking gentleman deliver a solid sales pitch, I could slowly feel myself falling into one of those "television shopping trances." Then the closer, "You owe it to yourself to have the financial freedom you and your family so richly deserve." Bingo. 1-800-whatever. Two weeks later, here are the tapes. What a country.

To my surprise, the seminar was quite good! I learned a great deal, though I never moved forward on becoming a real estate investor outside of looking at a few properties and having some business cards printed up. In all good conscience, I wish I could tell you that was the end of my seminar-purchasing adventure. It wasn't. It went on. Direct marketing tapes, more real estate. I even spent $1,000 on a weekend seminar at a local hotel. How interested does that sound in making a change in my life situation? Friends began to find out what I was up to. Having a Masters Degree in Communication from Michigan State University, I learned to tell people that I enjoyed "collecting" these seminars as a hobby. Spoken with just the right inflection, it even sounded somewhat intellectual.

Time passed. Things weren't getting any better. Others around me seemed to only augment the problem and not help solve it. I was running out of stamina.

Then I managed to convince myself that, for "management reasons," I would delve into motivationalism. Working at an ad agency, I had been exposed to these types of people through business communication meetings and sales seminars. With the utmost respect intended, I can honestly say that there are some excellent people in this lecture-driven field. Real "pump 'em up" kind of guys. Truly, I enjoyed watching them work very much.

So, on vacation in Florida one year, I bought a couple of cassettes "for laying on the beach." They were very good. Uplifting and insightful, "feel good about yourself" type stuff. Secretly, I needed to hear some of this. I was losing perspective. I was becoming "gerbil-ized."

Next on the agenda was my bout with the book store. I began to buy what I'll refer to as "coping books." Naming them wouldn't be proper, but you know which ones I mean. Time-management books, "meaning of life," "dealing with different personalities," etc. You get the picture. Chalk up another $500 in book store receipts. Suddenly, all this "help" was killing me.

I don't know exactly what made me do it, maybe the analyst in me, but I decided to go back through each seminar, tape and book and look for what I'll call "common truths." At first, I had no idea what I was looking for. Something. Some insight that I had missed. Some baseline that could serve as a "fulcrum" to get my life back into "balance." God, it was hard.

Over time, the scratch pad began to fill with bullet points. Not big revelations. Just points. Things like, "the most important time is spent in building a solid plan," and, "don't let the greed bug bite you." Some were more psychological like, "learning to 'reprogram yourself.'" Others were nearly religious, "God did not create you to fail." I'll bet I spent the better part of six months pouring over this stuff. Filling out my scratch pad.

Sometimes I like to have dinner at one of those revolving restaurants on top of a high building. From that perspective, under the spell of the shimmering lights, even the dirtiest, crime-ridden city looks elegant. It wasn't until I had a slightly different perspective on the contents of the now-full scratch pad that their meaning came through. I had always assumed the material would give me insights into them. The real insight was when I realized that the arrows were all pointing at ME.

Regardless of what you have been telling yourself for years, YOU are the only one that can make YOU do ANYTHING! I chose to go to college late. I chose my career. I chose to abide by the rules of the company. I chose to take their money. And make no mistake, only I could choose to change it.

What, in fact, had happened was a "refocusing." I learned to ask myself some very difficult questions. Not all of the answers were pleasant. But at least for me, I had started down the path of being more honest with myself. I had stopped blaming others and started accepting the responsibility personally.

Lesson #2

The only real control you will ever have is over yourself. Most likely, you will not change the basic pretext of the world. The good news is that only YOU can change the way you perceive it and, in turn, how you are perceived by it.

Chapter Three

A Line in the Sand

"Glory is fleeting, but obscurity is forever."

– Napoleon Bonaparte

The face that confronted me in the restroom mirror at work that day was distinctly different from the one that I had spent nearly 35 years watching change. From the first tooth, to the initial facial follicle, and then that hint of gray, this was a face that I had come to know even as time had stripped away the innocence. But today, I did not recognize the pain and frustration etched in the eyes and forehead. It was so completely out of character that I caught myself staring into the mirror to make sure that it was, in fact, me.

"If that dirty bastard does that one more time..." the soliloquy started, "I'm out of here." Sound familiar? You should have seen the wild expressions accompanying the delivery. I've heard that talking to yourself, more or less alone in an office john, is the first sign of insanity. I've heard the same said about starting your own company. But in my case, it was to be the first step in making a permanent change in my life. One that – I was certain – would make a positive impression on me, no matter what might happens. And you know what? The "dirty..." not only did it again, but it became a ritual of annoyance.

As a child, I hated vegetables. Name some. It didn't matter. The only possible exception was "black-eyed peas." Maybe because we only had them at my grandmother's house in Florida, once a year. So they became very special. It seems that special occasions make acceptable that which you may otherwise never do on a normal basis. The challenge is that the day-to-day world is not one giant special occasion.

Maybe it could be, should be. I know a few people who have the "gift" of making it seem so. But they are extremely rare and, unfortunately, I have not been one of them. To be sure, the Monday-through-Friday grind of the corporate business week, for me, was not a series of "peaks." For most people, the "peaks" occur after 5:00 p.m.

I've learned a great deal from my new daughter, Christina, especially when she was a toddler and it came to interpreting nonverbal communication and recognizing mood and attitude shifts. Most parents become quite astute at this. I could tell when she was not feeling well, when she was hungry, cold or just needed new pants. I began to watch very closely for signs, maybe even unconsciously.

I wish I had acquired that skill when struggling with the possibility of leaving my old company. Earlier, I talked about watching others for signs of lethargy and discontent. It seems that the most difficult person to watch, and understand, is yourself. In retrospect, the period was filled with little cues and changes that began to define the need for a new course of action. And, of course, the one that needed to see it the most, recognized it the least.

You know the guy who always comes in an hour early, "just to get prepared to start the day?" That was me in spades. Slay the business dragons, carry the corporate banner, and if you got "killed," be altruistic at all costs. Remember, this is the key to promotion. Our saying was, "We would run through walls for the client and the agency." It was with beaming pride that I would proclaim, "I have the best attitude in the building, bar none." But somehow, as the "walls" became less and less relevant, and the pain of crashing through them intensified, perhaps I began to question the motivations of the people directing the charge. The change occurred slowly, almost imperceptibly. My start time gained about two minutes a month, until one day I realized I was late for work. And it didn't matter. Sign Number One.

My father developed a trait early in his life that I truly did not understand until a few years ago. We'll call it "selective hearing." This most prominently displayed itself when he would try to watch a football game in the late fall when "us children" would be running through the house between him and the television. It was a wonderful thing to behold. You could speak right to him, as my mother would try, only to be completely ignored as if he was in a trance. But trip over your train set in the far bedroom, sharing his favorite expletive for pain, and he would suddenly appear in the doorway with belt in hand to "correct your language."

We all understand that in business, most people have "selective hearing," especially when they mess up and are about to look bad. Suddenly, they can't seem to recall that you reminded them five times to double check the figures before submitting the proposal. This seems to be SOP (standard operating procedure) in the business world. What isn't, though, is your reaction to it.

For me, it started out with my writing a few gentle reminder memos that "weren't really necessary," but just a follow-up. Then it became a matter of – my favorite word – "procedure." Over time, it digressed into "for the file" correspondence. Later, it was designed to "cover your ass." And in the final stanza, I was actually keeping a daily journal of all conversations and project status, "just in case." Sign Number Two.

All large companies, I would argue, from a personnel perspective, are microcosms of society in general. You have your party crowd. Your intellectuals. Your jocks. Your nerds. Etc. Inevitably, you find your circle of business friends to be much like yourself in a variety of attributes. Kind of sounds like high school, doesn't it? This is not to degrade the situation, but rather to acknowledge its existence.

It is very comfortable to be able to talk to people of your same genre when confronting challenges. Over time, however – again in retrospect – I began to form alliances outside the group to which I had been accustomed for so long. It happened in subtle ways. Mingling at company functions. Getting involved in other types of projects. Business trips. And the fabled, "let's do lunch." Somehow I couldn't understand how my "buddies could have changed so much." Obviously, they didn't. Sign Number Three.

It has been said that "no one grain of sand tips the scales, but rather the aggregation of all." I certainly believe this to be true. However, I do believe that every individual draws an "emotional line in the sand." One that has no tolerance for violation. I am not referring to that "dirty so and so" mentioned at the outset of this chapter. The line may be one of "personal goals for the future." Somewhere in our careers, most of us will come to the crashing realization that we are not going to be CEO. We aren't going to make a million-dollar salary. We are not the favored person of corporate management. The obvious question then is, "Now what?" Clearly, a tough question.

The proverbial "line in the sand" is what many of the seminar people refer to as "leveraging." Imagine a "spectrum of dislike" in my earlier vegetable discussion. On the left end, you may have, "Well, they're not so bad." And on the right, "If you make me eat them, I'll throw up and refuse to clean it up – no matter what." Movement along this continuum predicts action. The issue is, "How bad does it have to get, in your mind, before you take action X." To be sure, this is a function of the individual.

For me, when the level of discontent matched the number of challenges I knew I would encounter in starting my own business, the tradeoff and potential benefits suddenly made sense. Please understand that this intersection only occurs at very high levels. Just because you're angry with your boss or you didn't get the promotion, don't for a minute believe that you are anywhere close to the threshold. Emotional stamina and endurance are key attributes of the entrepreneur. In reality, knowing where your "line" is requires testing its upper limits. Few people you will ever meet can look you in the eye and tell you "they know."

Lesson #3

The key to leveraging action in yourself is full comprehension of the price of non-action.

Chapter Four

Skydiving Lessons

"Courage is grace under pressure."

– Ernest Hemingway

Once, I had a friend try to goad me into the "sanity optional" sport of skydiving. He was a good friend, but – thank goodness – a poor salesman. Appeals ranged from "the ultimate rush" to rather unflattering measurement allusions of a person's manhood. In the end, I decided to save this craziness for where it best belongs – mid-life crisis.

Though unpersuaded to indulge, I spent weeks thinking about the process as a whole. Looking back, the decision to start my own company had many striking similarities to what I had imagined the skydiving experience to be. And let me say this, although there is no substitute for direct experience, never negate the impact of "imagined or imaged" mental "dry runs." It has been shown that they can positively affect your performance and save you a lot of grief in the long run. One of my favorite sayings is, "I don't have to be shot to know that it hurts."

I learned this as a boy when I was involved with a swim team associated with the YMCA and later in summer camps at high school. Being smaller than most other kids my age, I found my way onto the springboard diving team. Here, I could compete with myself as well as with others and learn at my own pace...faster. One particular day, the coach had a movie of various dives, archive footage, circa 1951. But it didn't matter. The projector was designed to work equally well in forward and reverse. So for hours, it seemed, we watched the film and studied its many points of proper execution. This may not seem like much now with the high-tech nature of amateur sports today, but in the late 1960s, in Saginaw, Michigan, it was a big deal. Most importantly, it worked. Man for man, our diving team improved noticeably in the months ahead. And, as fate would have it, I went on to win a state championship that year. No brag, just fact. I credit my ability to visualize that film before each dive with giving me the focus and imagery to perform.

This is why, perhaps, visualizing the skydiving experience may have meant more to me than actually doing it. It forced me to consider each step in the process and analyze it independently and in combination with others. As I have said, the parallels with starting my own company were frighteningly similar. Here is what I mean.

Somewhere in the adventure of skydiving, you "get sold" on the idea in general. This is not as straightforward as it sounds. However the "selling" of the idea gets done – externally from a friend or internally by yourself – the decision to leap from a "perfectly good airplane," with a silk device strapped to your back, high above the ground, with the full knowledge that if anything goes wrong your chances of survival are slim and none, is made. You're "going for it."

In starting your own business, there is that day of reckoning. This is the moment when you come to the stark realization that your "line" has been crossed and it is time to change, or at least you cannot go on with the status quo. Hopefully, you won't die starting your own business. But there is a very real chance that you could lose everything you have built over your whole life in one fell swoop. One "jump" as it were. If you have a family or others who depend on you, this is family-decision time. And although the family may come to consensus, no one can take the burden of that decision away from you. You are in it alone. Alone, when you walk the floor at 3 a.m. wondering how you're going to make next month's bills, and alone when the client signs that first multi-million dollar contract. But in any case, you alone must make the "jump."

18

The next thing about skydiving is choosing a reputable place to take the lessons and do the actual jumping. My friend had a researched list of several places in the area. Most had instructors with military backgrounds.

In business, the parallel is in choosing the type of business to get into and where. If everyone listened to the statistics of how many businesses fail in their first year, nobody would try it. One critical issue is that there is a lot more to owning a business than meets the eye. When I worked in advertising, everyone outside the field would try to tell me how "glamorous" and exciting it sounded, and how lucky I was to have such a career. Admittedly, it did have its moments. But for me, the "moments" only represented about 5-10% of the time, and the remainder clearly overshadowed them.

The point I'm making is that I have had too many conversations with too many people interested in starting a business they "think would be great," but have very little practical experience in. In skydiving, the goal is minimal risk and maximum reward. The same is true here. My years in the ad business prepared me to start a business that was a logical extension of my interests and skills. It takes years to build a niche and credibility in business, more or less trying to "relearn" the entire trade. Many colleges selling night courses appeal to people changing careers with the term "retooling." In many ways, you're starting over from the beginning. And there is no shame in this. In the admission, at least you are being honest with yourself and realize how far back you need to go to grasp the basics of a new field. A female friend I had lunch with once said about my company, "The higher the wall, the farther back you have to go to get a running start to jump it."

I remember thinking about what it would be like driving to the skydiving school with my friend. Visions of macho rituals of "high fiving" and discussions of sexual prowess come to mind. Talk about "going big or going home" also played. But

19

the most striking thought was that of the anxious laughter and "butterflies."

For one very long season, I was on the high school wrestling team – for all of the wrong reasons – I might add. I got the living crap kicked out of me. Only won one match. The first. Scared to death and starving from trying to make my weight, the gym fell to a hush as my name was called. The coach, seeing that I was more likely to pass out than make it to the mat, grabbed me by the little ear protectors and slapped me right in the face. Dazed, the blood returned to my head and I pinned my opponent in 35 seconds. Never again was I ever able to capture that focused level of adrenaline.

Business is not about a one-time rush. It is a marathon of highs and lows. I was most definitely anxious and filled with butterflies, but these you must learn to control if you are going to win more than one match. For me, spending a year building a business plan, six months pre-testing it and telling no one in the process, minimized the "pre-game jitters." Somehow I stepped forth with confidence and focus instead of apprehension and doubt. The "school" can be a long way away, but make sure you are ready when you arrive.

The training for skydiving, or taking the lessons, has to be a lot of fun. All the "putting on the gear," "learning to jump and fall properly," and of course, the safety training. There must be a surrealistic quality to the process, in that preparation breeds confidence. Confidence in the fact that you won't die.

I'm a "gear" person by nature. I was the kid who always polished his spikes before every baseball game. One time, we got the chance to play at night and I put car wax on my batting helmet so it would reflect more light. Skill assessment and opportunity analysis is the "training" of the entrepreneur. Upgrading your experience bases, pre-testing, planning, etc. Remember, you may well be risking it all, so you had better be ready when the game starts. You only get one good shot.

Up until now, the potential skydiver has just been playing the role of "skydiver." But in my image of the process, reality must strike about the time you are told to "suit up." I'll bet I've put that chute on a hundred times, feeling every strap and buckle. Tugging on loose ends for a more secure fit. Sliding on the helmet, as if it might help. Ultimately, surrendering myself to the design and function of the gear alone. In a word, trust.

I have read that matadors in Spain go through a tremendous ritual of "suiting up" before a bullfight. The custom-made outfit is blessed for the safety of its wearer and gives the matador the feeling of being invincible. This, and his years of training, gives him the confidence to do battle with a beast that has the power to destroy him for a single error in judgment.

In the beginnings of any company, the "suiting up" process may well be the design of logos, completion of the business plan, development of initial advertising, office setup, merchandising trinkets, etc. In other words, the preparation. Testing is also critical to avoid stumbling at the start. Quietly find out how "it will play in Peoria," before rolling it out. In essence, build your trust.

For my birthday one year, my wife bought me one of the "try it and see if you like it" flight lessons at a local airport. So it is with vivid recollection of this experience that I can tell you about the next step in the skydiving adventure. It consists of three parts. The first is where you leave the office/hangar area and make that long (short) walk to the very small plane. Standing near the plane, it will shock you to realize that just two minutes earlier you thought this was a great idea, an adventure. But now, at the point where confidence and fear collide, the more rational side of your brain kicks in.

21

In starting my business, my "walk to the plane" came in the form of an after work cocktail with the head of agency personnel, who also happened to be a friend. I had decided that at this meeting, I would float the idea and watch for her reaction. As I sat alone in the restaurant awaiting her arrival, I knew that once the words left my mouth, I would have "boarded the plane." When she appeared in the doorway, I was actually trembling. Even though I knew it was the right thing to do, the reality of it all suddenly weighed heavily on my shoulders. By the end of the evening, the agreement was that I would make a final decision and call her by the end of the week. The decision had already been made.

In any plane ride, big or small, there is the infamous "wave" to those left behind. This is the second step. Safe on the ground, they return the gesture as if knowing something you don't. Some wave in sadness at your departure and wishing they, too, could be on board. Others wave with thoughts of "good riddance" and how foolish you seem to tempt fate in such a daring manner.

With my company, the decision to "go" was made before I even met her that evening and, for me, there was no turning back because I had already left, mentally.

Rolling down the runway, the third step, in a small plane, you feel each crack in the tarmac. As the engine roars and the sound made by the tires on each crack grows shorter in interval, your pulse races with excitement while your stomach churns with nausea. You're not really sure if it will fly. But no matter what is going to happen, at least you will know very soon.

For me, the "roll down the runway" was the last week I was at my regular job. It was an exciting, sickly feeling. Friends, although they wished me well, didn't ask me to lunch. I had no assignments, so the day progressed at a snail's pace.

Meeting attendance was not encouraged. And even in cleaning out my desk, I felt like a spy in deciding which files were mine and which should stay. I was now officially an outcast by my own volition, and it felt damn strange after so many years.

But perhaps, the biggest point in the skydiving process is when the wheels of the plane leave the ground. This is step three. Suddenly, there is no noise. No tires pounding on the runway cracks. No chatter on the radio. Only the rush of cool air in the side window that brushes your cheek, suggesting "everything will be all right." Maybe it is the cool silence and the gentle swaying of the plane that calms the soul. I'm not sure. But there is comfort.

Twice in my life I have left a company seeking change. Each was different. But they both had one striking similarity. As I walked out the door for the last time those Friday afternoons, I know for a fact that I did not turn and look back. My strides were strong and confident as I made my way toward my car in the lot. But it was as if I had lost control of my legs, they seemed to be moving for me – as if they knew something I didn't. I believe in destiny. And this day, although there was no going back, I knew that going forward was the only course of action.

Obviously, the moment of truth in skydiving is the jump itself. Maybe it is the sensation of falling that would scare me the most. Or knowing the worst-case scenario. But I think it would be the uncertainty of whether or not the chute would actually open. If it did, you would float softly down to earth with a spectacular view and some great stories. If it didn't, you would be able to consciously and knowingly witness your own demise, and there wouldn't be a thing you could do about it.

In starting my business, I had already jumped, mentally. That weekend was a wonderful time of celebration and rest. The stress was draining from my body as each minute took

23

me further from my past. I slept better than I had in three years.

That Monday morning started like hundreds of others. I got the baby fed and dressed. My wife dashed down the stairs and into the van, where Christina was already perched in her car seat. But with the aluminum "thud" of the garage door, there was a silence that I never will forget. It was like a bookmarker, clearly separating one chapter of life from another. As I sat behind my desk on that first day, and the reality of it all began to sink in, I remember saying to myself, "My God, what have I done?"

Lesson #4

Fear has two basic effects – it can either energize or paralyze. Preparation is the most reliable method of building confidence and reducing the fear associated with approaching the unknown.

Chapter Five

The "A" Bliss

"Twenty years from now you will be more disappointed by the things you didn't do than by the ones you did."

– Mark Twain

There is a period at the beginning of any company that is truly wonderful. There are so many things to do, decisions to make, people to call. Lunch with your friends is a must, of course, on your new corporate charge card. The printer calls you with your stationery. Your new computer gets delivered. People at the postal center learn your name. Life in general is like new love, and it is good.

This really is a great period for about three weeks. Maybe a month. Soon, friends are busy, or cancel for lunch. Your new supply cabinet is bursting at the seams. And over time, the phone stops ringing. I actually remember a particular week where I received no phone calls. Mumbling my way up the stairs that Friday afternoon I thought, "How can you have a business where no one calls?"

My wife and I are scuba divers, recreationally. We have made it a point to travel extensively in the Caribbean and Mexico, looking for interesting places to visit and dive. Having taken the certification training as well as maintaining a pleasant and accommodating attitude, we have been fortunate to dive in some wonderful places with friendly and knowledgeable guides.

The dive resorts we have been to have generally been great. Bright sunshine and crystal-clear water. The perfect place to relax. But in diving, too much relaxing or not paying attention can get you seriously injured. Each time we would set out on the boat for the morning destination, we would reestablish the "rules" of the day and remind ourselves to trust our gauges. (There is that word "trust" again.) One thing you study in diving is the physiology involved. Getting a classic case of the "bends," or decompression sickness, is not to be taken lightly.

To make a long lesson about dive compression short, it is about moving from one type of environment to another carefully and safely. Gases are exchanged and the body is "compressed" almost undetectably. That's the dangerous part. It is the slow return to the surface, pausing for your body to decompress at various intervals, that allows you to return to an environment to which you are accustomed.

This initial period in business, for me, was like learning how to exit one "compressed" environment and "decompress," preparing to enter another. If properly done in diving, there is no shock to your system. This is not the case in business. I vividly recall chasing around "being busy." In any company, scurrying about had the implication of productivity. It was also a means of measuring self-importance. You know these people. The ones who take their cellular phones into the restaurant and carefully place them in plain view of everyone within ear shot.

To me, these were all signs of "compression" sickness. And so that you don't get the impression that I am just throwing stones, I suffered from it 90% of the time. Further, so there is no misunderstanding, "busy" does not equal "productive." I know people, and so do you, who make an art form out of "baffling you with busy and not accomplishing anything."

Conversely, we have done the world somewhat of a disservice in having people believe that all issues can be "managed in a minute." All you seem to hear in business is "organizational skills," "time management," "top-line it," etc. I saw this strategy come apart in a meeting one day, when a person who had built a reputation for "handling"

26

everything you can imagine was stopped during a presentation. One of the management committee members, who was accustomed to rising stars, asked a rather probing question on a fundamental issue in the argument being made. A stunned and then embarrassed presenter was forced to admit only a superficial understanding of the material he was presenting. As I watched in horror, that instant taught me the difference between "top-lining" and "summarizing." These again are what I consider to be "compression" issues.

When you have your own company, you must learn to decompress and stop top-lining, guessing, assuming, anticipating, etc. And the downside of doing these things is simply different. You won't get fired, of course. You'll lose your house and family, credibility aside. Don't get me wrong. I am not suggesting that you slow to a snail's pace and do nothing. What I am suggesting is that you become more analytical, questioning, thoughtful, and strategic with each decision and project. You may only get one chance with a potential client to both get the job and protect the image of your company.

The weird thing about diving in very clear water is that your depth perception gets distorted. In just 100 feet of water, you can easily see the boat on the surface above. But objects are a lot farther away than they appear. If something would happen to your tank, for most of us, there would be no physical way we could make it back to the boat and safety.

In this early period of my company, profit and success were clearly visible. I knew the business plan was solid. Contacts were in line. Systems had been tested. We were ready to roll. But the feeling was like going to a fish farm without a fishing pole. I could see them jumping, but I didn't know how to reel them in.

This initial frustration, coupled with the first phase of decompression, for me, resulted in two things. First, a short, but impactful depression. I would get very upset when phone calls would not be returned. The more clerical burdens of the day became a nuisance. In general, I began to realize that the "boat" of success was a lot farther away than it appeared. And, that if something happened to my "financial tank," there was no way I was going to make it back to the "surface."

Second, it resulted in something I will call, "linear emotions." This is something that still has a tendency to nag me. In this "state," you have effectively minimized the "peaks and valleys" of joy and pain to a point where you become insulated so that nothing gets to you. Obviously, this is a defense mechanism. But at the time, you may call it words like "long-term perspective" and "even keel." What you really mean is that you weren't as prepared as you thought to face this different set of challenges so quickly. For me, this was a period that I managed to get through in short order, primarily because I had seen it one other time in my life. Earlier, I talked about knowing the "line or edge." In this case, the abyss. I know where my emotional "line" is. College taught me that.

Recently, I was riding home from the video store with a friend and somehow we got on the subject of college. It was with nearly moistened eyes that he described how wonderful his years at college had been. He recounted many stories of friends and frat brothers and sisters, parties, freedom and foolishness. These were the best of times. He concluded that "life would never be like that again."

Staring out the window, watching the shoulder of the road disappear in the sideview mirror, college recollection carried a whole different meaning for me. I had decided to go back to school after being laid off by a company I had worked at for six years. Depressed and nearly broke, with an associate degree I had earned at a local community college in helter-skelter fashion, I moved back in with my parents to really "go to college." No one, then or since, has understood the determination that lurked within me.

With student loan in hand, I met with a counselor, once. "Here's the deal," I said. "I want to get through my junior and senior year, get my Master's degree and write my thesis in 24 months." "Can't be done," was the response I got. With the list of prerequisites tucked neatly in my pocket, I had decided that it would be done. Twenty-three months later, suffering from physical exhaustion and on the verge of emotional collapse, the mailman delivered the Master's Degree Certificate with a 3.7 grade-point average. I did not attend the graduation ceremony. But I slept for two days.

The point here is an important one. It is not about self-aggrandizing. The "edge" is something you will experience in your new business. How you deal with it is the measure of your inner strength. Macho has nothing to do with this. This is about discipline, focus and resourcefulness. All of these things, once accomplished, add up to confidence. You will be on the road to success when you learn what the edge looks like and how to get back from it.

By the way, I'm not a member of my college alumni association. I figure that, since I had already given them blood, I'm not giving them money.

Lesson #5

Don't be deceived by the honeymoon period in your new business. Over the long haul, you will be tested both physically and emotionally. Learn your limitations to avoid a major calamity.

Chapter Six

Make Believe, Inc.

"Don't get the idea that I'm knocking the American system."

– Al Capone

I remember the day I bought my company answering machine at a local discount store. Consumer Report-researched and "on sale" made it the "smart buy of the week" according to the sign. Score one for the new purchasing agent in me.

But the relevance of this purchase didn't unfold until I got it home and set it up. With pen in hand, I began to scrawl down the "script" for the outgoing message:

"You have reached the personal office of Steven H. Brown, President of SH Brown Automotive Marketing, Incorporated. I am unavailable to take your important call, but if you'll leave your name and number, along with a brief message, it will be time-coded and forwarded to me as soon as possible. Thank you for your interest in SH Brown Automotive Marketing."

The strategy behind the message development had been considered for days. First, sound bigger than you are. Prospective clients don't need to know that you are a one-person shop until the time is right. Besides, everyone has an answering machine or voice mail. Second, name recognition is critical, twice if possible. In the ad business, our favorite term was "awareness," building awareness. Next, make the client feel important. Let them know that they have reached the "top guy" and that the "buck stops here." Fourth, make sure they know that you have a sense of urgency about returning their phone call. A quick editorial aside. One of the most unprofessional and annoying traits a person can have is not returning phone calls. It is simply another form of building self-importance and shows procrastination tendencies. So much for that. Finally, above all, be professional. Every act of unprofessionalism puts a nick in an easily damaged image.

Great. Ready to go. "I love it, let's do it," I thought with one finger on the "record" button...BUT...

The high pitched sound of the tape engaging somehow hit my mental "eject" button and out went all semblance of rational thought. You know the "MUTE" button on your television remote? It felt like someone had zapped me.

All right. Calm down. Rewind, set and...record. I had no sooner gotten to the end of the first sentence when anxious laughter rang out and I began to resemble a bit on a television out takes show. Each of the first 12 attempts all had the same effect. Finally, I did manage to get through it, poorly. For the next two hours, and after several coffee breaks, through what seems now like a hundred takes, I struggled to get a simple message into that machine.

Here are the two words that set the stage for what needs to be described in this chapter, "PLAY MESSAGE." Have you ever listened to yourself on a tape recorder? God, you sound goofy. Worse than that, your friends ask you, "what do you mean? It sounds just like you." Great. Couple this to the embarrassment level of wearing your underwear on the outside of your pants, and you begin to approximate the feeling I had in the pit of my stomach.

"Who was I kidding?" IBM, Shell Oil, these are companies, corporations. My "company" was just me, sitting there in my basement office trying to sound big. Sure, I'd read the books about "humble beginnings." But the driving sense of surrealism in my humble beginning was so overwhelming. Obviously, time for lunch.

The feeling began to haunt me beyond the answering machine incident. It was clearly a sense of misplacement. Sheepishness. It began to permeate other starting points of my business. Passing out the first business cards at social gatherings. Sending the infamous "cold-call letter." But nowhere was it so apparent, or so quickly brought to your attention, than when meeting old company friends and acquaintances. Those who knew you BC, "Before your Company." It was especially true when running into old bosses or superiors. These are the folks who not only questioned your sanity when deciding to leave, but – subtly or not so subtly – your abilities and skills.

As I think back on it now, it was the same feeling I had as a kid playing "make believe." Pick a game. It doesn't matter. Fort, army, cowboys and Indians, spaceman, whatever. The issue is that the game was only as "real" as you decided it was. You defined the rules of the game. You got to describe how the characters would look and interact. But best of all, you got to act out, through your character, your interpretation of how things should happen. In reality, how you played your role was a function of how you, or how you wanted to, see yourself. It was literally the first time you got to redefine yourself – free from external constraints.

Make no mistake about it. Although this was not play acting, it certainly was a period of "redefinition." In a nutshell, this was one of the most introspective, self-image redefinition periods of my life.

Up until now, it had been "image by association." Succinctly, you are what you do. Large companies depend on this to maintain order and discipline. Companies define the roles, and then you begin to define yourself based on the role you're assigned. Please don't misinterpret the intent here. Everyone needs varying degrees of structure. The issue is "from where does this structure originate and by whose design." Large companies spend millions of dollars building and protecting their image.

In the beginning of my company, I alone had the pleasure and responsibility of building an image, from the ground up. They said that companies take on the characteristics of their leaders, and for good reason. You may be able to fake it for a while, but you can't act forever. Sooner or later, the "real" you will show itself.

Perhaps the biggest issue in this period is coming to grips with yourself, as a person and as a new entrepreneur. Remember sitting on the floor, in the middle of the room, in your first apartment? For me, Martin Luther King said it best, "Free at last, free at last, thank God almighty, we're free at last." After the jubilation subsided, the next question was one of "Now what?" I can only wonder what the East Germans must have felt about their new-found "freedom" when the Berlin wall came down. I'll bet on "optimistic confusion."

Lesson #6

Redefining your own self-image – and building one for your new company – are critical elements in the long-term success of both.

Chapter Seven

Nickel Nametag

"As long as you're going to think anyway, think big."

– Donald Trump

Lawyers can be your best friend or your worst enemy. You get to pick. Sometimes they can be both. Personally, I like to be covered, up front, with contract wording, procedures, copyright and so forth.

While working out the details on my first big project contract, my attorney mentioned that her firm was having a "free" seminar on a set of employment issues and that she would pass along an invitation. Sure enough, two days later in the mail arrives an invitation, along with an invoice from our first meeting. So much for free.

The day of the seminar, I arrived as I usually do, about 15 minutes early. Big law firms can often be intimidating enough for large clients; for a "one person" company like mine, well, needless to say, I was justifiably apprehensive.

Be this planned psychology or not, I was greeted in the reception area by a woman who obviously recognized my name from the attendee list, once I managed to blurt out my introduction. "We're glad you could attend for your company, Mr. Brown," was her response. No other words she could have spoken, at that time, could have had a more powerful impact on me. Pure, piercing, supportive. Even though it was probably contrived, and the person delivering it certainly added to my male ego, it was the first time that another company or person saw me, truly saw me, as a company to be respected. Remember earlier, I talked about building an image from the inside out. Well, this was the first real feedback on how this redefined image was being received. And the positive response sure felt good.

The receptionist was standing behind a table filled with those stick-on name tags, the ones where you peel off the back. There, among other very recognizable companies, franchises, service businesses, retail shops and the like, alphabetically placed, neatly printed in magic marker, was a symbol that, for me at that moment, was of no less significance than that of the Congressional Medal of Honor.

Peeled and precisely positioned on my left lapel, the feeling was as if I had been "knighted." The nickel name tag had become my personal suit of armor. With out-thrust chest, I proudly accepted the honor for which I had labored so long. Of course, the receptionist was oblivious to all of this embellishment, and quickly greeted, in much the same fashion, the next person in the line that had begun to form behind me.

Entering the conference room, the coffee and morning "business pastries" were neatly arranged on a draped table at the far end, awaiting their first guests. My spirits and self-confidence were higher than they had been in 10 years. I was at my best from an open-personality perspective. I chatted freely with other early arrivers about silly "ice-breaker" type things: selection of pastries, decaf vs. caffeinated coffee, size of the conference room, and so on.

As the meeting began, I casually glanced around the room to get a feel for who was in attendance. One guy was a fast-food franchise owner (18 to be exact). A woman and her two assistants owned a secretarial business. (I'll bet you'd know them.) Another fellow owned one of the largest boat marinas in the area. In all, these were all some pretty big-time (for me) players. And there I was, sitting and chatting with people who had been through all of the trials and tribulations and were winning! This was a group that I aspired to be a part of.

Somehow, as we all left the seminar meeting that morning, I had a feeling of unspoken acceptance – or at least acknowledgment – by a group of people who had taken the risk, seeing that I, too, had the gall to go for it. That, in and of itself, was enough.

It is important not to confuse the purpose of this chapter – or period in my life – as one of ego-building and "rites of passage." Clearly, the point to be made here concerns the first real feedback or "inbound" response to my image-building efforts. The first real acknowledgment by "the world" that I was now something/someone that I built, and not just part of a company that bestowed an image on me.

Giving careful analysis of that feedback is critical to crafting, over time, the most powerful method of communicating your original strategic intent. To be sure, you will know rather quickly if your image-building efforts are on the right track.

Lesson #7

It is important to recognize feedback on your image-building efforts as quickly and as objectively as possible. This allows for any course corrections that may be required.

Chapter Eight

Five Minutes Over Brilliance

*"I don't know anything about music.
In my line you don't have to."*

– Elvis Presley

It has been said that the entrepreneur is the wearer of many hats. This is true. Unfortunately, they are of many sizes and don't all fit the same. This also assumes, by the way, that your head doesn't change sizes. But you know what they say about assumptions.

There was a particular week, not long after the legal seminar, that somehow had been scheduled by a masochistic secretary (me) that involved seeing each of what I'll call "critical assistance" groups. The business that I had chosen was one in which I felt very comfortable with my skills and background knowledge. I had studied hard, read a great deal and could converse rather fluently with even the best of my peers and colleagues. There was no denying a founded sense of pride. My confidence level was the highest it had been in a while.

The first meeting that week was with the accountant. As a high school and college student, I had always been good at math. I was one of those kids that thought trigonometry was foolishly straightforward. Calculus was far more difficult, but "fun" nonetheless.

In "real life," however, often the most difficulty you have is making sure you are not overdrawn at the bank. And that the IRS thinks you're a great guy at tax time. Really, it boils down to being detailed and disciplined.

While the majority of us have had to do company expense accounts to cover airfare, meals, hotels and a wide variety of client and personal "amusements," only the entrepreneur (besides the corporate accounting staff) is personally responsible to the government for properly compiling and submitting all pertinent business expenses. Remember, IRS agents, by nature, are rather conservative.

Being of a particularly meticulous (o.k. – even a little compulsive!) organizational nature, and somewhat computer-literate, I marched with head held high into the office of my new accountant. Under one arm was the neatly bound, tabbed binder with "1991 Business Expenses" displayed proudly on the front cover and spine. This man was exactly what I was looking for in an accountant. In the prime of his career, himself an entrepreneur, and meticulous, but personable. The kind of guy who, as a student, probably wore a calculator on his belt and had a pocket protector. And most likely hung out with more women than I did. Of course, that would not have required a great deal of effort. The thing I like most about him is his accounting "bedside manner." He rivals any of the doctors on television.

Perhaps that's why I was halfway home when I realized that for the last hour, he had in essence told me that I was an accounting fool. His analogy, close, but not a quote, was something like, "Your records are written in Russian, and now we have to translate them into a language that the American IRS can understand." Smooth, but in other words, you're stupid.

That's when our discussions of "chart of accounts," "deductibility," "wages" and the like suggested that my next stop should be at the library for an accounting textbook. Feeling more like a whipped puppy than a president, it was back to the office for a touchup on Accounting 101.

The second meeting was with my legal counsel. As I said earlier, a lawyer can be friend or foe, take your pick. I opt for "friend," spending the fees up front, hoping to avoid the "death by fee" possibility at the end.

Law was always one of those fields that kind of interested me as a potential career, until I took a few classes. Suddenly I realized that law was nothing more than heavily researched presentation skills. The side that could present the most persuasive argument, seemingly regardless of the facts or issues, was going to win. And the worst thing you can do is be – what the layperson would call – rational. That really screws things up. This is not good or bad, just fact. So much for my soapbox editorial.

This, however, does not negate the necessity of having your contractual act together when owning your own business. So, there I was. My attorney is outgoing and a pleasure to be around, yet the consummate professional. It was this combination of characteristics that allowed her to ever-so-gracefully suggest that perhaps my attempt at a first draft of the project contract was a "little unpolished." As she went down her mental checklist of "did you considers," I began to sink ever lower in my chair until the chair itself became optional from my final resting place. Even the questions on my notepad, that had taken days to compile, got stuck somewhere between my brain and my throat in an attempt to salvage some self-dignity. In other words, you're stupid.

The third meeting was with my insurance agent. By nature, I'm a "pound of prevention" type of guy. To be sure, entrepreneurialism is a risk-filled gamble, but a very calculated one in the most successful instances. Let's face it. It is easy enough to lose everything to circumstances that you can't control, so why not be covered for those you can.

Insurance policies, in general, bug me. First of all, they are written in a jargon that only a select few who have the power to reject claims can understand. Second, the type is too small, and somewhere, some hidden disclaimer is lurking. Finally, they always exclude activities that make life a little more entertaining, like scuba diving, flying a plane, etc. I realize you have to have them, but I would probably feel better if they would give me a toaster or something for signing up, like they used to do at banks. Every time I fly, my wife faxes her order form to the local Ferrari dealer.

Business insurance is absolutely critical to the small business owner. Unless your very future is at stake, you may not fight hard enough to win in the long run. Insurance for me became an emotional security blanket that gave me the freedom to "go for it," knowing that my family would be covered should it all "hit the fan."

My agent is a great guy, about my age. He is a "get to the point, what does it really mean," fellow who I have come to feel is genuinely trying to protect my interests and save me money. Maybe it's because his father founded the company, so entrepreneurialism is in his blood. In any event, they appreciate the needs and cash flow challenges of a fledgling company. They even gave me three "retired" file cabinets – my first – and it served to seal my affection.

In this particular meeting, both my agent and his father sat me down to "get me set up" with coverage designed to protect my business and myself. As we sat with coffee mugs in hand, the years of experience began to flow out onto the table, and soon my hand cramped from taking rather copious notes. The ugliest stories generally began with, "Once I had a client that..." The "moral" summarized the insurance need. Needs, by the way, whose obscure, but relevant nature had my head spinning.

I mean, let's face it. Fire and theft I understand. But the one that got me was "liquor liability." If I owned a restaurant, this would make more sense. But I'm a marketing guy. Why should I pay for this? The answer was clear when I heard the story. "Once I had a client who had worked for a long time to secure a big contract from an important client. Finally, they agreed on terms and decided to go out and have a cocktail to sign the deal." Is this sounding somewhat familiar, so far? "While at the local watering hole, the festivities got rolling a little too fast and the client simply over-indulged. Refusing a ride home, he then proceeded to wrap his car around a tree. Although not killed, he was severely injured and sued the business owner for millions, and won." The moral, as carefully explained, was that one moment of jubilation led to the demise of the business since the owner was not covered. Thus, liquor liability.

By this time, they had the papers in front of me and I knew that they had my best interests in mind. The fee was reasonable, and with the stroke of a pen, I was covered. As I listened to the sound of my footsteps echo in the parking garage, I was struck with a sense of numbness. Certainly I knew insurance was important. But I didn't know how important. As the key went into the ignition, I remember saying to myself, "How could I be so stupid?" When the parking garage attendant barked out "Buck fifty, please," it snapped me out of my daydream. "I'll need a receipt."

The fourth meeting was with my financial planner. We've all heard horror stories about people who have trusted a planner with their life savings, only to be devastated at retirement time. I am determined that this will not happen to me. The definition of money and its utility has changed for me in the past several years. Maybe I'm becoming more of a realist. For one thing, I firmly don't believe that Social Security will be around when I get ready to retire. Just look at the demographic numbers and the national debt and I'll bet you come to the same conclusion. Further, in the '50s, people joined "big companies" for the long-term security of it all. But, with companies selling off divisions, outsourcing, reducing benefits and the like, there really is no security. This is not to suggest that these moves by companies are not done for solid financial reasons. I'd probably do the same thing in their positions. But, that does change my position.

The real reason, I believe, that I started my own business was not about the money. Sure, everyone has visions of grandeur. Make that million. But for me, it was more of a sense of shaping my own destiny and being able to control my lifestyle. Believe me, in a large company, people above you do not have your best interests in mind as they make decisions that directly affect your salary, benefits, lifestage or family situation. Now clearly, that is a sweeping generalization. There are many outstanding companies that do go far above and beyond the call of duty for their employees. God bless them. But they are in the minority. So for me, money became the means to a lifestyle end and not the end in itself. It serves only as the "lubricant" in the machinery of it all.

My financial planner knows this about me. He also knows that I have the patience of a monk and the tenacity of a terrier once I get an objective planted in my head. Of course we talked about the various levels of the "planning triangle," and all the other "technique" issues of planning. But as an entrepreneur, I now have needs that are different from those that I had working at my old company.

In this meeting, we were scheduled to discuss a rollover into an IRA account. The financial planner, too, is a great guy. Understanding, but coldly blunt. I like that. As I began to lay out my thinking on the issues, I remember he smiled and sat up in his chair. "Please don't take this the wrong way," he said, "but you need to concentrate on how to best spend your money, not save it, in this early point in your company." This was from "Mr. Long-Term Savings and Investment." He explained that I was in a building mode and that, by definition, is expensive. Stay as clean as you can from a credit standpoint, but do what you have to in order to get the business off the ground.

Needless to say, I felt like I had just taken a curve ball for a called third strike. This was exactly the opposite of what I expected him to say. The elevator ride down two floors took two weeks. Why was it taking me so long to "change gears" about money? Maybe because I had so little. Or maybe I didn't know what to do in the first place. How could I be so stupid?

The fifth meeting was lunch with a lady who used to work at a research company that was directly related to the field I'm in. I happened to talk to her on the phone one day, and we agreed to swap stories and insights about our marketing experiences. So Friday lunch seemed like the perfect opportunity.

An auto dealer in Phoenix once said to me, "You know, I really enjoy working with smart people." Boy, this is true. Unfortunately, he wasn't talking about me. But the point was made. I really like listening to an expert in their field. Maybe it's because of their confidence and poise. Or the fact that they don't have to pretend, because they truly do know what they're talking about. In any case, I love professionalism.

This particular meeting was set up so that she could give me some pointers/insights into how to gather data more quickly and cost efficiently. When I arrived at the restaurant, she had already beaten me to the table. Early – already I'm starting to like her. As I followed the hostess to a small table in the middle of the room, I couldn't help but wonder how our skills and backgrounds would match up. "Steve," she said, rising to shake hands. Articulate and well dressed, she represented the image that most companies would kill for.

As we began talking, it became clear that this was no marketing lightweight. Her background and knowledge of the data was as solid as anyone I had ever talked to. She was also keenly aware of the politics and difficulties that only an "insider" could know. Further, the scope of her dealings was broad enough to include virtually everyone in the industry, domestics and imports. This was a much coveted gem.

As the first hour passed, I felt myself slipping into a "learning mode" as the notepad had found its way onto the table. This lady knew her stuff and it was both refreshing and humbling.

Walking out to the car, I had a sense that I had a lot yet to learn about marketing and data collection. Over the next several months, I found myself calling and meeting with as many people in the field as I could to improve my skills. But, pulling out of the parking lot this particular day, one question lingered: "How could I be so stupid?"

There was a stool, in a particular establishment, on this Friday afternoon that beckoned me like a siren. Its allure was greater than a fresh baked apple pie and more comforting than your muffy slippers after two weeks on the road. As I sat there recapping my numerous notes from the week, I was reminded of the adage about wearing different hats as an entrepreneur. On Monday, the hats were all too small. By Friday, they were all too big. And none of them had changed size!

Learning about what you don't know can often be more important than reestablishing what you do know. Don't be afraid to find out. "Another JD and water, Mr. Brown?," quipped the barkeep. "Hold the fruit" was my reply.

Lesson #8

Being an expert in your own field is only the price of admission in the entrepreneurial game. You must become proficient at a variety of other skills if you are to operate and protect yourself and your company.

Chapter Nine

Table for Dinner, Party of One

"The nice thing about being a celebrity is that when you bore people, they think it's their fault."

– Henry Kissinger

I wish you could have seen my face and been in my chair the morning the phone rang with the approval of my first official assignment. It was a small project, as projects now go. But it was the first, and that made it special. On adrenaline overload, I spent three days pulling out all the stops. When the "rush-rush" project was in the binder, I couldn't wait to make the client presentation. This was to be an informal "across the desk" type thing, no big deal. The meeting went great and everyone was very pleased. It was 10:15 a.m. on a cold Monday morning.

Trying desperately to contain myself until I got outside the building, once there, soulful laughter erupted and I was beaming from ear to ear. You would have thought I'd just won the World Series. I couldn't wait to tell my wife. My fingers flew over the buttons on the car phone. Ringing, ringing. "You have reached..." Damn it, the answering machine. Pick up, please. Oh, forget it.

Undaunted, I racked my brain to think of someone I could tell that might share in my joy and actually care. But in the middle of a Monday morning, your options quickly become limited. Slowly deflating, I found my way to a local donut shop close to my office. "Would you like cream for your coffee?" asked a graying waitress named Wanda. Explaining the reason for the big smile on my face, she peered at me with those mothering eyes and asked, "Did you say sugar raised or nutty?" I knew then that the need for celebration I was feeling would have to go on hold. Slumping slightly on the stool, I chose the "nutty."

Lessons present themselves in strange ways and, this day, I had learned another important one. It was about the isolation of the venture I had undertaken. Some nights, I would dream that I was lost at sea on a raft. This was not a bad dream per se. The sea was calm and the weather was great. But the feeling was of cold wet rubber on my back and hot burning sun on my face. There was that slapping sound of the waves against the side of the raft. And only the clouds to keep me company.

The reality of the situation was quite different. I had my wife and daughter, friends, associates, freelance employees, vendors and suppliers, accountants and lawyers, on and on. In essence, I found myself surrounded by people. None, however, could share the burden of decision making or take the blame. As a company employee, if you run into a question or challenge, you always have the option of asking your boss or peers. As an entrepreneur, there is no up, or down for that matter. You have heard the old saying, "It's lonely at the top." Well, believe this, "It's isolated on your own."

In thinking about the experience as a whole, a lot of other activities I was involved in at the time were similar in nature. I started back jogging to stay in shape and get out of the office. With no full time employees, the days were spent working alone. Building the resource files. Designing the direct mail campaign. Purchasing supplies. Early morning breakfasts. And of course, writing this book. Please understand that I am not suggesting that this is horrible, just fact.

All of the time spent by yourself makes you very introspective. That has its pluses and minuses. But on balance, the experience either teaches you to shoulder the burden and move forward or it presses you into social withdrawal, which as a business person, you cannot afford. At first, it's scary. Fear, they say, either paralyzes or mobilizes. You can't freeze up. One of the tangible manifestations is over-analyzing everything. "Analysis paralysis." As they used to say in school at the end of a timed test, "pens down." Make a decision and move forward. But in this case, you are the decision maker. Although I hate all those clichés, expressions like "the buck stops here," are absolutely true. Over time, you will learn to enjoy the decision-making process. What you will learn to deal with, however, is the sense of emptiness in the isolation. You may become cynical or somewhat paranoid. Don't panic. These, too, will pass.

There is an obvious danger in sliding too far off into isolation. It could affect your marriage or relationships, push your friends away, and in general you might lose your perspective and sense of humor. One thing I caught myself doing was revisiting old hangouts, "just to see if they had changed." Once I went back to an old rock bar we had frequented 15 years ago. Although the remodelers had been hard at work, there was no doubt that it was the same old place. Even more scary was the fact that the same BAND was appearing all these years later. Headed toward the door, the lyrics of a '70s song stuck in my mind, "The strong pick up and move on. The weak give up and stay."

The key to this period for me was learning to transform emotional isolation into objectivity and not alienation. In graduate school, I had toyed with the idea of staying on for a Ph.D. One of the jokes was that the only real reason anyone would bust their butt to get one was to be greeted in fancy restaurants as "Dr. Brown, party of two." As an entrepreneur, whatever your educational background, you must be prepared to accept the fact that no matter how many people attend, emotionally, it will be "table for dinner, party of one."

Lesson #9

The isolation of being an entrepreneur must become a positive decision-making position, or you run the risk of slipping into myopia and/or depression.

Chapter Ten

Social Chameleonism and the Art of One-Downsmanship

"If I had done everything I'm credited with, I'd be speaking to you from a laboratory jar at Harvard."

– Frank Sinatra

There will be two days you will remember in your life when it is all said and done: the birth of your first child and the day you get your first check as an entrepreneur. Come to think of it, these events have a great deal in common. They are both physically and emotionally hard as hell to bring into this world, and a God's joy once they are here.

I remember the first time I ever got paid for working. My grandfather "hired" my cousin and me to dig a large pit for one of his off-the-wall projects. We were all of seven years old. It took us 10 hours a day for a whole week. When it was finished, we had to climb out with a ladder. We both got 10 bucks. My grandparents lived in a small town in northern Michigan. The town had a "Dairy Queen," at which we spent the next three hours and every cent treating ourselves like royalty between feasting and pinball. To give you some idea of how much damage this was to a seven year old, these were the days when you got a quart of "softy freeze" on a nickel cone. We're talking major ice cream consumption.

As we waddled home with stomachs bulging, our change in lifestyle was about to be short-lived. My uncle met us at the door and we proceeded to get one of the sternest lectures about financial responsibility I can recall. He was absolutely right, of course. We had acted foolishly, from his perspective. But for a couple of seven-year-old boys who had worked their hearts out, nothing that could be purchased for $10 would have matched the pleasure.

A friend of mine who is a successful entrepreneur, once said to me, "Party hard when times are good, for they may be short-lived. Party hard when times are bad, 'cause it may get worse." I guess this is the adult version of a trip to the "Dairy Queen."

The day the first check came in the mail was like the time – as a child – I sent away for one of those plastic submarines that worked on baking soda. In both cases, the eternal (four weeks) wait, precipitated a dance not unlike a Kenyan tribesman after a successful hunt. All of this took place in my driveway – in plain view of the neighbors. It was 2:30 in the afternoon.

Dispensing with the "civilized" letter opener, I ripped open the envelope to find those wonderful words, "Pay to the order of SH Brown Automotive Marketing, Inc." In my trembling hands, I held more money than I have had in my savings account for most of my 36 years. It wasn't the biggest check I had ever been involved with, but I'll bet it was the most important. I felt acknowledged. There was pride in knowing that I had "marketable skills," that someone else was willing to pay for services I could provide, independently. To be sure, for the many business people, actors/actresses, athletes, etc. who already make their livings in this fashion, they will smile and find this hopelessly sappy. But for people who have spent their whole lives being indoctrinated in the American corporate culture, this newfound enlightenment takes on a whole different meaning.

This feeling affects you. It changes the way you carry and think about yourself. It forms the foundation for a new type of confidence. In line at the bank, you'd have thought this was just an everyday occurrence. But inside, I felt like I had just transcended into true "businesshood."

The ride home from the bank affects you as well. You are caught in the mental crossfire of "not letting the greed bug bite you," and "How can I make this happen again as quickly as possible?" I can see how it quickly becomes an addiction. Not to the money, necessarily. But rather to the feeling of accomplishment. This began to seed itself in my head as the initial stage of a complete redefinition of what it was to be "successful."

The next morning stirred with a renewed interest in a rather sparse appointment book. Energized from the previous day's events, I plunged into the cold call list, "drumming up new business." Days turned into weeks and at best I had scheduled a few "let's get together and chat" lunches.

As time rolls away, the need for money and the feeling of accomplishment begins to erode some of the "higher ideals" you had written in your business plan. You start to widen the scope of your service capabilities. No matter what the request, your first reaction is to respond, "Sure, we can do that." You begin trying to be all things to all people. Instead of being true to yourself and staying with the plan, you tend to change "colors" as a function of the environment you have just entered. Your judgment can be more easily clouded. You may make a decision or two that is definitely not in the best interest of your company, long-term.

Another thing I caught myself doing was "over-killing" the service function, to the point of being a pest. I have long suggested that learning the "art of one-downsmanship" was the key to a successful service business. But there is no honor or money in over-servicing a client so as to turn a positive into a negative. Lack of money or projects on your part does not constitute an emergency on their part. We have all heard the business saying, "If you need an answer now, the answer is no."

A kind boss once said to me, "People don't do their best thinking when they're running their mouth." He didn't have to draw me a map on that comment. But I took that advice to heart when struggling in this period. I began to take more notes and LISTEN to what people "meant," not just what they said. It is important to remind yourself that you spent over a year writing and testing a business plan that was meticulously designed for a reason. To stray from it this early in the game is like throwing away the playbook in football on the first set of downs from scrimmage.

As in most businesses, a copy of that first check hangs in a frame on my office wall. When the calls get tough to make, I take it down and stand it up behind the phone. The whole time I am talking to a client on the other end of the line, I am focused on the power of that small paper and its ability to change my life. What most people don't understand about the entrepreneur is that the vast majority of us did not go into business for the money. Most, like me, wanted a change in the quality of their lives and a more personal sense of accomplishment. Further, they are not "thrill seekers" or "daredevils." The risks that are taken are calculated ones based on researched issues and high potential return on investment.

Above all, you have to be yourself. Trying to please everyone pleases no one. Besides, it is too hard.

During a capabilities presentation one day, a potential client asked me about our abilities in an unrelated aspect of the business. The most credibility I ever built with an individual in the first six months of our operation was when I told this person that we didn't provide that type of service because we weren't qualified. A somewhat sleepy meeting suddenly perked up when the client sensed the fact that we were "for real" and that we could be trusted.

Lesson #10

Flexibility and humility are essential to getting a new enterprise off the ground. However, trying to be all things to all people simply won't work. Consistency is the key to building initial credibility.

Chapter Eleven

Planning Aerobics

"Find something you love to do and you'll never have to work a day in your life."

– Harvey Mackay

Have you ever watched those aerobics programs on TV? Here's the scene. Several shapely young ladies and very toned young men bounce their way to physical fitness at a location that is usually the director's vision of nirvana. Generally, the marketing people make sure these programs run in the morning and at lunch. This makes the most of the guilt experience. The message in all cases is very clear: "We're young, beautiful and sexually attractive, and you're not."

When I was with the ad agency, we were on a TV commercial shoot in northern California when the power of these shows made their greatest impression on me. A cold morning rain greeted us at 5:00 a.m. as we assembled in the hotel parking lot to get a short briefing on the day's activities. As the steam from my tightly clutched coffee cup fogged up my glasses (I always wore my glasses after a late night solving the world's problems with the car prep guys), I heard someone in the crew remark about how the only people awake at this hour were those watching the early morning aerobics program from San Francisco. After several "colorful and creative" comments, we got on with our day's work.

The next morning looked better from the bedroom window, but chilled us all with temperatures in the high '40s as again we huddled together in the same parking lot. But this time when the subject of the "morning aerobics" program came up, virtually everyone in the group, crew members, cast, lighting gaffers, directors, clients, agency people and, of course, me, could describe each of the "routines" in vivid detail. Few recalled actually doing the exercises.

The point to saying all of this is that often when you think that you are the only person in the world with a given interest, challenge or set of circumstances, you find out that many others have the same circumstances if you just get them to admit it. Or, you may be shocked by the self-disclosure of others in the "proper" setting.

I had convinced myself that most entrepreneurs had found "the secret to success" and had carefully planned the path that best capitalized on it. This is what I believed when I was an employee in the "corporate world." You may believe this, as well. To my amazement, I have found that a lot of independent business people don't even have a formally written business plan. This shocked me in as much as I labored for nearly 18 months – beginning to end – to build a "solid" plan to follow.

Having a plan definitely has its advantages, and some negatives as well. I ran into a period, as all businesses do, where sales calls – and more or less sales – became difficult. It seemed that there was some invisible barrier that I didn't understand how to get through. I tried a variety of approaches. I was relentless in attacking what I had planned as key points and people. All this to no avail.

One evening, frustrated and beginning to doubt myself, I sat down and reviewed the "plan" that I had labored to build. After several hours, it became apparent that I had overlooked an area that held what I'll call "tier two" business. With renewed enthusiasm, wild pencil markings and profit calculations changed not only my perspective, but the plan itself.

Interestingly, I did manage to get some more sales calls and a project out of that night's activities. So as business slowed again, it was "back to the plan" for another look. This time, however, I was not as successful at finding increased opportunities. But, some "minor modification" was in line.

For the next couple of weeks, these latest changes resulted in even more calls, even more rejections, even more "planning modifications." I actually got to the point where I had a "plan of the day," in the form of daily "to do" lists. Don't get me wrong. I'm not knocking these as an organizational technique. But, when they themselves become the plan of action, you must recognize that you have difficulty. The challenge is that the "exercise of changing the plan" can become an excuse for not making the tough sales calls. You are simply putting yourself through the "aerobics" of procrastination.

What all of these changes effectively did was to create a very real self-doubt about my original instincts and calculations. Suddenly, I was unsure of the core essence of my business and found it difficult to articulate just what SH Brown Automotive Marketing was in business to do.

Planning and plan modification is critical to any business. But the written document is created to get you to organize your thoughts in the first place. If you have built a business plan, then somewhere in your conscious or subconscious mind you have come to grips with what you need to do. The revenue streams. The avenues of fastest growth. Key contacts. And perhaps, above all, a sense of timing, making sure the quality of the product doesn't falter so that you maintain credibility overall. If you do go back to review the core plan, do so as a "yardstick" to measure progress in key areas. I have found that it cannot become the gold standard of success or failure.

My sister once asked me about starting a business and so I decided to show her my 400-page business plan. Somewhat overwhelmed, she said, "I'm not sure if I have the energy for all of that." Certainly, that was a fair point of view. But it is my belief that the "planning exercise" is designed to strengthen "mental muscles" that, in the marathon of starting your own business, will provide the energy and stamina necessary to "tough it out" when things get soft.

My old junior high football coach once said, "During the game is not the time to practice." Once the business plan is finished is not the time to start doubting or second-guessing its utility. Flexibility is vastly different from a fire drill.

Lesson #11

Having a business plan is an absolute necessity, not so much in defining the "answer," but rather to organize and focus your direction. While the plan should be reviewed and modified based on success and failure, it should not be shelved in times of difficulty.

Chapter Twelve

Shades of Green

"Always forgive your enemies.
Nothing annoys them so much."

– Oscar Wilde

In the summer of 1976, a close friend and I decided to take his new van to Florida for a cheap vacation. With a full cooler in the back seat and the tape deck blasting, we left Detroit in the early evening and did the "drive all night" routine, straight through to Daytona Beach. When we arrived, it was late in the afternoon and we were both dog tired. But with more enthusiasm than brains, we parked the van down on the beach, unloaded the lawn chairs, and settled in for a brief nap. It was wonderful. Sand, surf and sun. The next thing I remember was this wet feeling on the seat of my pants. Startled, I suddenly jumped up and realized that the tide had come in while we were asleep. Not only were the chairs getting wet, the water was about to enter the open sliding door of the van.

People on the beach who had been watching this take place were hysterical. We must have looked like the "two stooges" trying to get the van out of the ocean. Once successful, we were greeted with applause and the whole show was over.

Clearly, subtle changes can occur when your attention is distracted that may be so slow and lulling as to make them imperceptible. One of these changes you will encounter in starting your own business is in people around you. As I have said earlier, change is, of course, a two-way street. With a new and challenging endeavor on your hands, you will be forced to deal with conditions differently than you

61

have in the past. Others will no doubt view this as "acting funny" on your part. And generally, they are right.

But the focus of this period is the rather stark realization that "something is up" with others around you. The best analogy for the feeling is that everyone else was in on a joke, except me. For some reason, I had the same paranoid sensation and I became very self-conscious of what I said and did. But here is the kicker, I didn't know why.

In chapter 10, I talked about "social chameleonism." This was not a new concept for me over the course of my life. As a child, my family moved a great deal as a function of my father's changing   job assignments. It was rare that we would be any one place for an extended period of time. In today's society, this is a very commonplace occurrence.

The net effect of this on children, I believe, is to force them into one of two directions. Either the child develops a very powerful self-image, independent and assured, or they very deeply desire to "fit in" because they are constantly struggling to do so. This last situation always keeps the child on the outer fringes of the social circle. The bottom line is that as a person, you are either one who forces the situation to adapt to you or you learn to adapt to the situation.

I fall into the latter of these two states. Knowing this has taught me to be resourceful and self-sufficient. But more importantly, it has taught me to recognize changing situations before others. To be sure, this is a broad generalization. It does, however, bring me to the point.

The point is that as a entrepreneur, you must be both strong-willed enough to force situations to conform to your specifications and be adaptable enough to recognize and integrate yourself into dynamic environments. The first of these was something I had to learn. And it did not come easily. Others of you will have to learn the second point. That will not be easy, either.

Learning to be somewhat stronger willed and molding a situation to your own image first requires that you have a defined image to mold to. I'm sure psychologists will go ballistic when they read this. The issue though, for me, was that moving in this direction required a purposeful attitude change on my part. Crassly put, it was about learning to "walk the walk and talk the talk." Please don't misunderstand this. I am not talking about arrogance or obnoxious over-confidence. What I mean is a newfound inner strength and optimism that allows you to transcend the difficulties that you will encounter. Again, this was a learned situation for me and an important lesson at that.

Because I had to change my attitude and core inner-strength belief systems, this was a side of me that few people had seen before. It was foreign territory, at best. I am convinced on the one hand that this is how "it" started. But over time, other "forces" began to work.

The "it" I am referring to is what I perceived as subtle changes in those around me. This will happen to you, as well. "It" starts out with cute little comments. Harmless. Simple. Things like phone messages on your business answering machine wanting to "speak to the president" from your friends and family. Lunch questions like, "How is it really going" for you. Uncomfortably long pauses after you hand a friend you haven't seen in a while your business card. "Courage" comments after people recite new business failure-rate statistics. Left-handed introductions at social gatherings. This is how "it" starts.

Competition between people is as natural as growing old. By starting your own company, you will have taken a giant step forward in taking control and changing your life. There are millions of people who simply cannot do this for one reason or another. With these people, you will suddenly be an outcast. Don't expect to win a popularity contest with your old friends in the short term. And the only way you can "go home" is to fail at your new business and try to fit back in to their perception of what is right for you. To be sure, this is unfamiliar ground and one that will not be comfortable, at first.

Perhaps the best way I can describe both my childhood and entrepreneurial experience is in the word "transition." You suddenly find yourself between the life others want for you and the one that you want for yourself. A few years ago, my wife and I moved from one house to a larger one across town. As the truck pulled away from our old house, I was struck by the fact that our entire lives were rolling down the street in the form of a 40-foot tractor trailer. One fire, at this point, while we were "transitioning" would have wiped us out. An uncomfortable moment, to say the least.

We really loved moving into our new house. We busted our butts to get it. Saved our money, worked hard, all that kind of stuff. But you know what? Years later, most of our friends still haven't seen it. And those who did in the early years implied that it might be "a bit much" for such young people.

The nut of this discussion is that you may find no one really wants you to succeed in this world...but you. To step out of the mainstream and "walk against the wind" is a lonely proposition. Your efforts will be chastised, mocked, victimized by jealousy, sniped at emotionally, and, unfortunately, derailed in some cases. Consider these to be tests of your personal inner strength. If being financially secure and independent was easy, everyone would do it. It's not, and they aren't.

You are the one who will agonize over the money at three o'clock in the morning. You are the one who will face tough clients and projects. You are the one who must bear the responsibility for all aspects of your company. And you are the one who can, therefore, pridefully offer your family a new and better life than if you hadn't taken the challenge.

64

Achievement is a very personal thing. Having your own company is not the only expression of achievement and is certainly not for everyone. But, if it is yours, then you have the right to feel pride in conquering its many challenges. And you need not apologize for it.

On the wall in my office I have, in a small frame, is my personal "adopted" philosophy from Rudyard Kipling in the poem "IF." One of the passages tends to sum up what I've been trying to say in this chapter. It goes like this:

"If you can wait and not be tired by waiting,
Or being lied about, don't deal in lies,
Or, being hated, don't give way to hating,
And yet don't look too good, nor talk too wise."

Lesson #12

The entrepreneurial journey is about change, and change is not easy or comfortable. The trials you will face inherently require that you must adapt to the tasks at hand. However, it is important to remember that others may not be as supportive as you would expect.

Chapter Thirteen

Spring-Loaded Doors

"Don't be afraid to take a big step if one is indicated. You can't cross a chasm in two small jumps."

– David Lloyd George

Any business starts slowly. Inevitably, there will be sales lulls. What you do during these periods will mark you as a long-term success or short-term failure. This section is not necessarily about time-management skills, although I do have some thoughts on the subject. Most business people have been exposed to books, seminars, lectures, etc, by people who attempt to help you get your life in order. This will no doubt cost you a pretty penny. I have a cheaper and more permanent solution for you.

Over the Christmas holiday in the first year of business, my wife's mother became ill in Florida. After a quick decision to have my wife and her sister drive down from Detroit (no flights available), I suddenly realized that I would be alone with our nine-month old daughter...for a week. You want to talk about time-management skills? Every executive in America ought to have – or be refreshed – in this experience. The downside of course is that a lot of lecturers would be out of work, the economy would tumble worse than it has, and it would all be my fault. What else is new?

Our initial lull was a substantial one, four months to be exact. No work, no income, nothing. Having predicted this possibility in the planning process, I had been wise enough to slash and burn all expense budgets to the bone, so the monthly debt load was minimal. We made no capital expenditures, shut down all "out of town" travel and were real happy we had not signed a lease agreement on the copy and fax machines. In all, we had anticipated and were prepared to "ride out a storm" of considerable duration.

This is not to suggest, however, that everything was "hunky dory." The first problem was between my ears. Coming off a very successful first quarter, I had gotten very "used" to being busy and getting paid for it. At first when things got quiet, it was a welcome change. I could refocus on financial, update our information files, and review our job costs analyses. That went on for about a week.

On the Monday of week two of the lull, meetings were being canceled and postponed at an alarming rate. The problem in my head was one of perspective. I started to get angry, take it personally when things changed. I've always been a calculated fighter. I think most entrepreneurs are by nature. We hate to lose. But, when you lose perspective, this can be a substantial negative. Fighters, when directly challenged, have a tendency to "kick it up a notch" and get aggressive. Pro athletes talk about playing at "a higher level."

In business, on the supplier side of the fence, this can sometimes be viewed as "pushy" or "difficult." If it goes too far, you can quickly get the label of "pain in the ass," and no one will want to meet with you. And even if they do, they will be negatively predisposed and will do so "just to get it over." The result is that both of you have wasted your time.

Tuesday saw me slip into this "higher" level mode. The entire week was one of calling and re-calling, scheduling and rescheduling. At around 3:30 p.m. on Friday, I hung up the phone with an insight. Let's just say that I had been "huffy" with a certain secretarial gatekeeper who was particularly astute at her job. She had just professionally deflected my fourth try to get on her boss's schedule and my patience had expired. Bad move. The insight was, "Hey stupid, you're supposed to be representing your company's image to these potential clients. Remember them?" These are the folks you want to pay you for your product.

The key is that clients and potential clients don't give a "tinker's damn" about your situation. They couldn't care less about your urgency to keep things moving forward. And clearly, it is not their job to conform to your schedule. Many of you will be saying to yourself, "We already know this, how basic." True enough, but swimming lessons can be pretty far from your mind when you are drowning. When your life depends on cash flow and you don't have one, things can get murky.

My grandparents in Florida had a screen door on an old porch just off the kitchen. It was the main thoroughfare between the backyard and the dinner table, so you can imagine the abuse it took from "starving" grandkids. On one yearly visit, while I was still very young, the old door had been replaced with a brand new one. After chasing dogs and rabbits through the green orange groves of summer, the call for lunch penetrated the trees like a cool breeze. The sprint down the two-lane dirt path allowed for maximum velocity heading for the kitchen. The plan was to blast through the door as we had done so many times before. But this time, the worn and rusted springs were gone and the weight of a 40-lb. child proved to be no match for high tension steel. I now fully appreciate the feeling an insect has when being swatted by a giant fly swatter. Dazed, but not really injured, I remember my grandfather's leather-like and stubble-bearded face writhing in laughter with tears streaming from his eyes. "Boy," he gasped, "how do you like my new door?" I learned something that day about the power of spring-loaded doors and the physics of "equal and opposite reactions."

In the world of sales and service, there is no doubt that aggressive, persistent and tenacious tendencies play a significant role in success. By no means do I consider myself the quintessential salesperson. It is a skill, an art form, that I am trying to acquire. But I have learned this: planned pressure is far more successful in the long run than brute force. And you can never lose your perspective and composure. There is much more at stake than meets the eye. As the owner of your own business, you alone set the standards by which all else will be judged. You wear the "image target" around your neck for all to shoot at.

Please don't misinterpret what I have said to suggest passive "doormat-ism." You simply can't operate your company by sitting around and wringing your hands. You'll starve. What I am saying is that this period is one of composed consistency of sales effort. Panicking won't help. Sometimes, the harder you try to force a situation, the worse it turns out. The more you push, the greater the resistance. Remember that door. If you are not careful, this can be a major spiral into frustration, especially as money challenges pile up.

I managed to escape this spiral quite by accident. You won't have to. The key to what I am about to say runs contrary to the base entrepreneurial spirit that is the desire to "do things yourself and maintain some semblance of control." To break out of this period, you have to reach out for a new perspective and some networking help.

I had lunch with an old friend and former client from years back at an "off the beaten track" restaurant. It was wonderful. We spent three hours reminiscing, and she was very interested in what was happening. Somewhere in the conversation, she recognized my current frustration and began to investigate further. In the most genuinely concerned fashion I can recall, she reminded me that no one is superhuman. You simply can't do it all yourself. She repeated a story that I had originally told her in an advertising strategy presentation about the effect of third-party credibility and persuasion. As her words poured out, a new perspective was beginning to emerge.

That evening, I was on the phone with a person with whom I had previously worked. This individual was very well "traveled" in the industry. We met for breakfast and he wanted to hear about my company and who I had already contacted. Mind you, this is a person who was NOT a potential client for me. Think about it. You know these type of people. We talked for about an hour. Just before he left, he said, "Got a pen?" For the next several minutes, he listed people I should contact on his referral. Scribbling at Mach speed, I noticed that his connections were at the very highest levels of management in these companies. The best part was he volunteered to "lay some groundwork" on my behalf. The rest was up to me.

My postal bill that month reflected the quantity of names on that list. My appointment book reflected the quality. In the final analysis of it all, our fourth-quarter profits were mainly comprised of business from that list.

People count. The right people count more. This was a principle I had obviously forgotten...until now.

Lesson #13

No matter how difficult things get, you must never forget that you are in the "persuasion" business. Attempting to force yourself into a situation in an overaggressive manner will only damage matters long-term. Networking is a method of enlisting the persuasion skills of others on your behalf.

Chapter Fourteen

The Rule of Divine Intervention

"Someday you will stop praying for business,
get off your knees, and start hustling."

Terry L. Butz, President,
Terry L. Butz Creative, Incorporated

While watching the TV news one evening, my heart poured out for survivors of an airplane crash who were commenting during an "on location" interview. One woman in particular described the scene inside the plane by saying that "people were in a state of mortal fear." She said that there wasn't a lot of panicking, just praying.

It struck me that high degrees of stress tend to drive people to look for "strength" beyond that which is currently at their disposal when they come to grips with the reality of human frailty. Those of us who have been fortunate enough not to have been in a similar situation can only imagine what goes through a person's mind in times like these. Perhaps it is only the soldier who could discuss this subject with expertise. Because, unlike "victims" of disastrous circumstances, the soldier, with forethought, premeditatedly enters the unknown with training and courage, but most importantly, with faith. A belief in some greater destiny.

I believe that there is a place for this concept in the entrepreneurial arena. There will be a point at which nothing you will try will work. In writing this, I am recalling a specific four-month period. Your bank accounts will be very low, if not dry. There will be no business on the short-term horizon. Suppliers' invoices will continue to arrive. Something at home will demand extra money, which you won't have. The pain, frustration and isolation may be more than you have ever had to endure.

After building my company business plan, neatly typed and bound, I wrote these words on a blank page in magic marker: "God will not fail me if I do not fail myself."

Herein lies a key issue for me in my business and my heart, and that is a driving sense of "destiny." As corny as it may sound, I can't recall a time when I didn't truly believe that a greater "force" was guiding me. The sensation is one of being "led" – or more accurately, dragged – through trials and tribulations that I have no rational reason for enduring. No one in their right mind would have conducted themselves as I have in many instances. That means things like always being the one to volunteer for the tough assignments. Some people might say that I'm a loner, or just enjoy the battle.

My message to you here is that you must be prepared, through events in your life, to endure physical and emotional pressure unlike any other. And the challenge might not be so bad if you were completely alone and had literally no other responsibilities. But for the person who is reading this book, spouses, children, family, friends, more or less employees, clients, suppliers, etc. can add significantly to the pressure.

What exactly does "not failing yourself" mean? In a word, discipline. And here is the weird part. I don't mean obvious things like returning phone calls or attending meetings on time. That's just pure professionalism. And if you don't have that, you don't have a chance anyway. What I'm talking about are the details of your life that affect your attitude and, ultimately, your behavior.

In week three of this four-month period, I became aware of subtle changes in my behavior and actually jotted them down on a yellow legal pad that my daughter used for coloring. There had not been an "inbound" business phone call in seven working days. Embarrassed as I am to admit it, I actually called the phone company to "try" my number to make sure it was working. The lack of external stimulation had directly accounted for the first several points on my list.

First, I realized that I was getting to my desk about five minutes later each day. You may think, "Well, that's no big deal, especially since you work out of your home. No morning drive on crowded expressways. No lukewarm coffee spilled on your lap. No searching for a parking space." But think about it for a second. Five minutes times 10 days is almost an hour. So instead of starting at 8:30 a.m., now you're talking 9:30 and headed toward lunch. This might be tolerable if you had just returned from a five mile jog or returned from the health club. But in this case, it was simply a question of resetting the alarm clock. While I don't believe in a lot of set rules, here's one. Never reset the alarm. If your business opens at 8:30 a.m., always be ready at 8:30 a.m. Your clients are.

Second, I noticed that my choice of attire had gone from suits and ties, to casual slacks and sweaters, to jeans and, finally, to running suits. The real comedy is in the rationalization. "I started my own company so that I could do what I wanted to do. And if I feel like being 'casual' today, then fine." What a crock. This is just a tangible manifestation of you feeling sorry for yourself. That one big opportunity can slip away if you have to tell a client that you "can't come right over because you have to change." Click. Now serving vendor number two, your competitor. And I defy you to get back on that client's phone list. Get ready every morning like you are about to give the biggest presentation of your life, because you just might.

Just an aside about being ready. In junior high school, I was nearly the smallest member of the football team. Each day at practice I would intentionally try to do something to get noticed. My specialty was the blocking dummies. It was actually kind of fun and there was no chance of them retaliating in the locker room. One particular day, my skill at punching out inanimate objects got noticed. The team's fullback had twisted his ankle. Over the sound of colliding shoulder pads and the high pitch of a training whistle, I heard the coach call my name. "Brown, get in there." In all honesty, being third string, I didn't know shit from third base about what I was supposed to do.

"When that guy comes through the line," said the coach pointing to a guy somewhat smaller than a truck, "you knock him on his ass." While the direction was crystal clear, there was a certain numbness between my ears. With the shriek of the whistle, my first "play" was happening. Being as small as I was, the fellow that I was supposed to block never saw me, and a crisp shot to the knees sent him crashing to the ground and me as well. Digging the clinging sod out of my face mask, I felt a swift slap on my back. "Helluva block kid, way to sacrifice your body." For the rest of that season, I would find myself "sacrificing my body" while others ran for touchdowns. But it didn't matter. I was a starter, and it felt good. Always be ready. You never know when your shot will come.

P.S. Being in the right place at the right time landed me the highest-grossing contract of my first fiscal year. It was one of those "crash and burn" projects where you strategically position the blinds to keep the sun out of your eyes as it appears over your computer screen – for the third time in seven days.

The final behavior change note had to do with my growing social isolation. My appointment book began to fill up with personal lunches that often included cocktails and lasted two hours or more. Not only was I not getting work, but I was systematically eliminating the possibility to do so by wasting the contact time. Please don't get me wrong. Everyone needs friends to talk and gossip with. However, as a new business person, you must reach out and talk to as many prospective clients as you can. This is your job. Contrary to popular belief, no one else on this planet cares if you succeed or not. You alone must care.

You have no doubt surmised by now that the common thread to all of these behavior changes is an erosion of focus and discipline. The challenge can be exponentially increased if you have a home-based business. This translates into easy access to all the distractions. After a month of no income or business, you'd be surprised how interesting the laundry can be.

I made a pact with myself that in writing this book I would stay away from a bunch of "lists." This chapter gives me my greatest temptation yet to cut loose with "do's and don'ts" to control your focus. But in the interest of "purity," suffice to say that a morning and evening routine concentrated on professional/personal appearance and efficient operations will get you through it. This will vary from person to person.

The idea of "not failing yourself" has another interesting aspect. Simply put, it is the image you project to others. This has the obvious components of confidence and enthusiasm. Confidence, I am persuaded, is about 90% preparation and 10% personality. We've all heard the expression that "information is power." Information then, is the superstructure of confidence. The point is to make sure you are a voracious reader of trade journals in your field and can articulate the latest point of view on the hot topic of the week. I have found that with people's schedules, you have a powerful advantage just by staying current.

The other aspect of image is enthusiasm. I had spent the better part of a year pursuing a client that I felt very strongly about. The hunt had cost me hundreds of presentation dollars, with no contract in sight. While I was packing up my gear after presentation number seven, one of the key players came back into the conference room and said, "I know we haven't given you the contract yet, but be assured we haven't given it to anyone else either. And that's because we're not talking to anyone else but you. We just love your enthusiasm and determination." Eight weeks later, they became one of the best and most prestigious clients we have.

I started out this chapter talking about "destiny" and greater "forces." Maybe I believe in destiny because I feel that through discipline and focus I can help build it. When times get tough, and they will, you are going to have to draw on all the skills and stamina that God gave you if you are going to make it. In the meantime, you need to learn how to reduce the amount of luck required to make your business grow.

Lesson #14

While faith may give you the path to destiny, only self-reliance and diligence will take you down it. Let faith be the "icing" on the hard work "cake."

Chapter 15

Swimming at Night

*"Basic research is what I am doing
when I don't know what I am doing."*

–Werner von Braun

I have a scuba buddy who is not only a close personal friend, but the Chief Engineer at one of the largest automakers in the country. Without question, he is one of the youngest-thinking, most progressive people I have ever known. The irony, however, is his complete mastery of "climbing the corporate ladder." We have all heard the old adage, "If you want to get along, you have to go along." My buddy has learned to accomplish the first, without being handcuffed by the second.

One weekend in both our busy schedules, we planned a short adventure to a place that neither of us had been, Penetanguishene Park, Canada. The novelty of diving there came in two distinctive aspects of the water: fresh and COLD! Both of us were relatively accomplished divers, and the allure of a new challenge was impossible to resist.

The point of departure was about three hours north of Toronto to give you some idea of the terrain and climate. After a seven-hour drive from Detroit, we were anxious to meet up with the rest of the dive party and stow our mountains of gear aboard the "live-aboard" dive boat named the "Baccus Diver." I later learned that it was named after the Roman god of orgies or something. With a name like that, you can well imagine the personality of the captain, freewheeling Captain Ken.

Captain Ken was the epitome of a "salty sea dog" that had seen it all in his 30-plus years in the Canadian Navy. And while it might have been "Canada's underwater park," it sure as hell was Ken's boat. When he first came down the ship's ladder from the bridge, wearing a light beige jumpsuit and sandals in 52-degree weather, we knew that this gray-haired fellow had been around the block once or twice.

In all, there were 11 divers. Captain Ken gathered us all up in the main dining room around 8:30 p.m. and served up the rules for the weekend aboard ship. With a roar of the engines and the smell of diesel, we left the dock around 9:00 p.m. in complete darkness. Only the full moon and the ship's lights reflecting on the water broke the blackness. It would be a two-hour ride to the first anchoring point where we would spend the night.

The cabin was abuzz with the sound of gearbags being unpacked and sleeping bag zippers. It reminded me of a floating mobile home. Small, bunk-like sleeping quarters were the norm and yet, because of the limited number of divers, there was plenty of room. As my buddy and I were stowing the contents of my "necessities" bag, Captain Ken appeared in the dimly lit, narrow hallway just as a 40 oz. Crown Royal bottle was thrown on the bunk. I remember watching Ken's stern, rugged face begin to melt into a devilish smile, and with twinkling eyes he said, "Looks like we know who the leaders of this group will be."

After several "getting to know you" casual exchanges, it was back to the bridge with Captain Ken. We decided to take a "catnap" while the ship made its way up the coastline and headed out toward open water.

Static commotion on the ship-to-shore radio and the revving of the engines were sure signs that we had reached our final destination. The cold night air came in through the open porthole and slapped open my eyes. As my buddy and I lay tossing in our respective bunks, the remainder of the dive group sat sleepily at the dining table, clutching their coffee mugs.

"Well, we're here. Who wants to dive?" was the taunting call from the bridge. One by one, each resident of the dining table found a convenient reason why a night dive was not a good idea. All, that is, except for us. "We paid money to dive, so let's get wet!" was all the motivation I needed to hear from my friend.

The outside air temperature was 52 degrees as we began the lengthy process of wiggling into layers of wetsuits, gloves and hoods. This was the first week of September, but the water was a chilling 58 degrees. As we stepped out onto the dive platform at the stern, the moon cast a magical glow on the water.

A small island lay off the port bow. Just below the boat, in 40 feet of water, was the wreck of an old wooden sailing ship that went down in a storm in the late 1800s. Checking my dive lights, my imagination conjured up a ghostly image of tattered sails and cold raging seas. In a few minutes, we would be exploring the decks of that very ship.

It was about 1:00 a.m. when the hissing sound of our regulators broke the evening silence. Of 11 divers, we alone went into the water. As far as I am concerned, night diving is one of the most eerie, yet rewarding experiences in scuba diving. It is nearly impossible to describe the sensation to someone who has not done it. Leaving the security of the boat, you knowingly jump into complete darkness. It is a very foreign and frightening environment. Bobbing around in the small chop of the cold water that evening, I was struck by the overwhelming sense of dependency on the training and the gear that could be the difference between elation and disaster.

But the real difference between diving at night versus in the day is the game your head plays with you. As my buddy and

I swam down the keel of the "Baccus Diver" just below the surface, the lights and the shadows it caused made it seem much larger than 60 feet. Visibility was about 10 feet. This meant that there were points in our descent down the bow line where you couldn't see the bottom or the surface. Actually, the only thing you can see is what appears in the beam of your lights. That limited vision, combined with wondering what is lurking just outside the beam, is what kept the others on the boat.

Suddenly, out of the darkness, appeared the shadowed bow of the wooden sailing ship. Frozen in time and resting ever so quietly on the sandy bottom, it loomed above us as we explored the many interesting secrets that lay within. It was covered with small crabs feeding at night. Teeming with activity, it was a sight that was simply not available to the daytime diver. The flash from our underwater cameras looked like lightning. And the soft silt appeared as a velvet cover. All in all, it was the highlight of the whole weekend.

Back on board, the wind had picked up slightly, sending the wind-chill into the 30s as we struggled to remove wet and cumbersome gear. Donning our synthetic longies and jogging suits, we sat at the dining table and toasted our success with, what else, Crown Royal. It had been a once in a lifetime experience, and we were the only ones to have done it. Here's to us. "I like you guys already," said Captain Ken, emerging from the tiny galley with a handful of cookies. "Now get some sleep."

During the night, the wind direction had changed and in the morning, the sun shone brightly through my east-facing porthole. The banging of pots and pans shattered the gentle slapping of waves against the side of the boat. While we staggered to our feet, the strong smell of coffee and ship's gruel filled the air. The rest of the dive party was now up, fed and ready to go. At Captain Ken's morning meeting, it was announced that the groups' first dive location was "right below us." Excited by the story of its demise, the group quickly gathered up their gear and headed for the dive platform. All, that is, except us. We had already seen it at its finest. There was no hurry to see it mundanely again, although we did, later, during the day.

From that moment on, we were clearly different from the group. Separated by a sense of adventure, it endeared us to Captain Ken and differentiated us from the others. For that brief weekend, we "had the right stuff." And it felt good.

So what does our scuba weekend in Canada have to do with the subject of this book? Plenty. I have struggled to articulate how entrepreneurs differ from others and why it seems so right for me. This particular adventure solidified the difference. Most folks could never force themselves to drive seven hours to a place they had never been, in a foreign country, sail two hours out onto a body of water they can hardly find on a map, suit up in scuba gear in 50-degree weather and dive in...AT NIGHT. They might, and did, with a group of others, with supervised leadership and DURING THE DAYLIGHT. The difference is as simple as – here comes the cliché – night and day. (That was cheap and I apologize.)

But starting a business is like swimming at night. It shouldn't be any different from swimming during the day. It is the same water. The same swimming technique. The same challenges. But it is! At night, with limited or no visibility, it is a frightening and sometimes paralyzing thing. Your confidence fades when you are alone in the cold, black water. You begin to distrust the skills and equipment that you have always relied on. And you can find yourself isolated and panicking. God knows what is lurking in the water around you.

As a new entrepreneur, your greatest fear is that of the unknown. Who will be my customers? How will I be able to purchase equipment? What will my competition do? Learning how to productively deal with uncertainty and trust the skills and abilities you possess is the most important thing you can train your mind to do.

You must learn how to be comfortable with only seeing what is in the "beam of your light." In other words, controlling the things that can be controlled and dealing with the others.

In a nutshell, as Kipling once said, "...trust yourself when all men doubt you, but make allowance for their doubting, too."

Lesson #15

Starting a company is not so much about courage as it is about a sense of adventure. It is the difference between being a "passive recipient" and an "active participant."

Chapter Sixteen

Coffee Mugs

"People will buy anything that is one to a customer."

– Sinclair Lewis

It was 7:15 on a gloomy Wednesday morning as I sat on the rock-hard reception area couch anticipating a long-awaited 7:30 a.m. meeting. Needless to say, this potential client was a "morning person." You know the type. Up at 5:00 a.m. Three- mile jog. Granola breakfast. And that famous "A"-type personality speech, repeat after me, "I'm too busy to meet with you during office hours, but if you really want to see me, I make 7:30 a.m. appointments." Everybody in business knows someone like this. I am not putting this down, mind you. But this is either a person who has nothing to do with small children in the morning, or has a spouse who doesn't work. Whatever.

I had tried all of my standard tricks for coming out of the morning haze. Slowly, the fast food drive-through coffee was having an affect. Just then, a young receptionist emerged from the "almost a kitchen" and inquired as to whether or not I would like something to drink. "One leaded mega java with a cream chaser," was my feeble attempt at an ice-breaker. Less than amused, she efficiently disappeared only to return with the standard Styrofoam offering. The steam rising from the surface reminded me that presenting with a scorched upper lip was not the best image-building opportunity. When I put it on the table to cool, she smiled demeaningly. After all, she "had gone to all the trouble to chase it down."

Moments later, the shrill, high-pitched tone of the intercom signaled that my long-awaited "pow wow" was about to begin. As desperately as I tried to anticipate what would happen next, the severity of the vice grip handshake caught me off guard, and the impression left by my college ring was still clearly visible 30 minutes later in the car.

This was an important client to me. With one swipe of the pen, my fledging company could have been off to the races. Scrambling to recover from the aggravated assault to my right hand, I blurted out some trite opening line just to get the conversation started. "Do you believe the weather we are having?" was all I could come up with. "Hell, what's a little rain?" he loudly responded. "Why, when I was in the Navy..." was the preamble to a 10-minute lesson in "macho" at its finest. Having satisfied his ego, he then proceeded to "get down to business."

"While my sources tell me that your firm does very good work, I'm struggling to see a 'fit' within our company to use you," was the terse attempt at a quick blow-off. I was more than accustomed to hearing this from certain people, and my retort came in its well-rehearsed format. Quite frankly, it stunned him a little. Somewhat off guard, he asked more probing and encouraging questions. And all at once, I realized that the "wall" was slowly losing some of its bricks. Did I realistically expect it to fall completely in that meeting? Of course not. But my mission had been accomplished just by developing the first "crack."

After about 25 minutes of receptive exchanges, it was clear that today's efforts had been concluded. One of my former bosses had a great line for getting me to shut up once we had made the sale. "Let go of the pump handle son, the bucket's full," he would say. In this case, truer words could never have been spoken. "I know you're a busy man and I have taken up enough of your valuable time," was my shot at making a clean break. But before I got the chance to close my note pad, thank goodness, he said something that affected me so much that I wrote it down verbatim. "Steve," he said, "I like your spirit and work very much. But you must realize that you are not the only one out there providing this type of service. While the other folks in this organization like to meet and talk with you, frankly we get busy and, well, forget you're out there in the heat of battle. You know, out of sight, out of mind."

There was tremendous insight to be gained from those words. But at that very instant, it escaped me completely. I thanked him politely and, after a pleasantry to the receptionist, I shuffled off to my cold, wet car. It wasn't even 8:15 a.m. and I had already "taken a curve ball for a called strike." A little off balance and somewhat dazed, there was only one thing to do – get donuts.

My "less than energetic" strides were quickly picked up on by Wanda the waitress. By the time I had made my way down to the far end of the counter stool, looking "challenged by a quandary," she had a nice cup of coffee and my "I don't get it" nutty donut all set up. I pondered the words he had spoken for at least half an hour. "My God," I thought. "I can't call him every day or he'll get all hot and bothered. I've given them my sales material and business card. And there is only just me. I don't have a salesperson to help me yet. How can I get their attention when I'm not there?"

Sliding down off the stool, I waived at Wanda and headed for the parking lot. In the slot next to me was a relatively new, red 4x4 pickup truck. It was obvious that its driver was in a hurry based on the angle at which it was parked. The engine was running and the driver's-side window was almost completely down. A passenger, propped up against the window on the far side of the cab, worked feverishly to get his morning fix of nicotine. The radio blared out the latest tunes on the "new country" radio station.

Up to this point, nothing unusual had struck my attention. Until, that is, I noticed the dashboard of the truck. There, resting ever so snugly in an after-market cup holder, was a pristinely clean white coffee mug. Its stark contrast to its surroundings held my attention for several seconds. But the real interesting part about it was that it had the country western radio station logo tastefully printed on the side. Do you think that...? Sure, it had to be. As the truck's passenger looked over at me, I darted inside my car to avoid staring.

You may be saying to yourself, "So what? I see that all the time." That is exactly what I thought driving back to my office. But something continued to nag at me about that damned mug. And then it hit me. The mug's owner, somewhat out of character perhaps, seemed to care for and maintain that object a little better than others in his possession. It was obvious that he enjoyed listening to the station on the radio. But even without the music, the mug reminded him of something he enjoyed doing. Even if the radio was off and he was out on a job sight, that mug was working overtime at attitude readjustment. That type of "silent salesperson" was exactly what I needed.

It would be more than fair to say that times were lean. I hadn't sold a job in months. Expenses, while carefully controlled, continued to eat away at the bank book. Now was not the time for a big capital investment. I had $358.22 in the company checking account. The obvious temptation was to "pull in my horns" and do nothing.

Old-adage time. Remember the one about, "it takes money to make money?" Me, too. But I didn't have any money. So, now what? Then I recalled a certain New Jersey auto dealer who spoke candidly to me about being in business for yourself at a management training seminar at the Wharton Business School. "Money," he instructed, "and your use of it, will often test your commitment to what you believe in. If you are not willing to take a calculated risk, then you really don't want or believe in what you are doing." He went on to say that, "Anybody can be bold with someone else's money. But, when your name is at the top of the check, you get to know firsthand about confidence and inner personal strength."

The issue was clear. I could sit by and do nothing, thereby guaranteeing my continued lack of success. Or, I build a plan to get things rolling, get off my butt, and do it. Hoping has never gotten a single piece of business for anyone. So, I got busy.

That evening on an artist's sketch pad, I started analyzing each of my clients. Once, a person called me "compulsive" and I had to look it up in the dictionary. For every single meeting I have ever been in, I have taken rather copious notes. These are done afterward in a quiet place so that I can really think about what was said. The notes are punched and bound in a 3-ring binder. This evening's analysis was made much easier based on these records.

After several hours, a couple of clear patterns began to emerge. Perhaps it was simply a function of the type of business I am in, but most meetings were held before 10:30 a.m. Lunches were frequent. And, nearly all clients, if nothing more than for the social courteousness of it, would offer me coffee regardless of when the meeting was held. Maybe I looked like I needed the caffeine. Further, in watching how the clients interacted among themselves, it was clear that most "shop talk" and meetings were conducted over and around the coffeemaker. The die had been cast.

The next morning, my fingers flew over my rolodex and found the number of one of my old buddies in the merchandising game. You know, "trinkets and trash," as it is often crassly referenced. I hadn't gotten 20 words into my predicament when she said, "No problem, you need high-quality coffee mugs with your logo on both sides at the 'good guy' discount." Precisely. Thirty seconds later, my order was being faxed to the supplier. Two weeks later, I would be the proud owner of 144 porcelain salespeople. "I'll send you the invoice once I receive the confirmation from the supplier," was the next thing I heard on the phone. "Oh, by the way," she said, "the total is $647.85. This is really a great buy, don't you think?"

While I had gotten what I wanted, I only had one small difficulty...money! The mugs cost twice what I currently had in the bank. But one thing was for sure: at least I was trying to make SOMETHING happen.

It was a bright, sunny day when the call came in that my magnificent mugs had arrived. With all the composure of a five-year-old in a toy store, I dashed over to pick them up. Upon my arrival , two huge boxes rested in the corner of the small office. One of the boxes had been opened for inspection. With the fanfare of a fluttering lip drum roll, came my first glance at the brilliance of the first-time "merchandising czar." They were beautiful. Gleaming white, with my yellow and black logo. Truly a point of pride and a sight to behold.

We couldn't find a two-wheeled hand cart, so instead, we loaded each box on a rollable conference chair for the long trek to the parking lot. I'm sure people driving by wondered why we had two chairs in the driveway by the look on their faces after we were done loading the boxes. Driving away, I had a renewed respect for the mailroom that often got overlooked. Now, I was the president and mailroom.

I carefully unpacked each one once back at my office. But then I was struck with the second challenge. What was I going to put them in for delivery? The phone book was the answer to this question, and a local packaging store had just the small decorative box that I was looking for. A little white tissue paper for effect, and the whole package was coming together quite nicely.

But something was missing. I couldn't quite put my finger on it. My goal was to make this special for the recipient, and the gift needed that little extra "oomph." One evening, the idea struck me. In each box, I would place a little verse that tried to give its reader the inspiration to be more progressive in their approach to new ideas and challenges. The selling proposition of my small company was based on a different approach to "doing the business." So it seemed quite appropriate. The verse read like this:

CHALLENGES

It's easy to find a reason NOT to strive for goals...
To put them aside for a week, month or year.
Soon, time steals the desire
And the greatest challenge is in living with the regret.

With the package now complete, I began making appointments and delivering the silent salespeople. Ad guys reading this book will shake their heads and say things like, "That merchandising, awareness-building gag is the oldest game in town." True. And for the marketing professional, it is relatively old hat. But when it is your image that you are building, with your money and your name on the door, you have a tendency to protect it with much greater zeal.

I can't tell you with any certainty that I have sold a single project to date from those coffee mugs. But I can say this, receptionists and secretaries, all of which were on the distribution list, remember my name and I always get a better appointment schedule because of them. And recently, I even saw the verse I had written pinned on the bulletin board at one of my clients. Here is the kicker. At the beginning of this chapter, I told you about the 7:30 a.m. client. Months later, I had a second appointment with this fellow. Much the same scenario with an interesting twist. This time, when the receptionist offered me coffee, it came in MY mug! Score one for the guy in the "trinkets and trash" hat.

Oh, by the way, some of you are asking, "Hey, how did he pay for those mugs when he told us he didn't have the money?" Nice to know that you're paying attention. When I had originally ordered the mugs, I asked about the terms of the invoice. It was just after the first of the month and I learned that billing didn't occur until the END of the of the month, so I had 30 days there. The invoice, when it arrived, was payable NET 30, which gave me an extra month. In essence, I had 60 days worth of credit on the mugs. And remember what I said about confidence. I was sure I could sell something in that period of time...and fortunately enough, I did.

The key here is that, even when times are lean and you can't afford to do much, to do nothing is the surest way to guarantee failure. You must MAKE things happen.

Lesson #16

When you are just starting out, there is no way you can be everywhere at once. Merchandising is a method of keeping your name and logo in front of potential clients and key contacts when you are not around.

Chapter Seventeen

Learning to be Stupid

"Why isn't there a special name for the tops of your feet?"

– Lily Tomlin

The sound of the telephone shattered the deafening silence as I peered numbly out the window not long after a Mexican combination plate lunch. It was like a dream. Everything was happening in slow motion. I was so tired that it took all the strength I could muster to answer it. "So what did you sell this morning?" was the shock that stung my left ear. It was my entrepreneurial friend who I hadn't spoken to in quite some time. "I just wanted to call and see if you were feeling sorry for yourself or what."

"Are you shittin' me," was the most macho and combative retort I could muster on such short notice. "Things are rockin' and rollin' man." I would no sooner have told him I hadn't sold a job in four months and that I was on the brink of financial disaster than to stick my hand in a garbage disposal. "That's great," he said. "I'd hate to think you were out of leads, frustrated and nearly broke." My gut just wrenched. How could he know? "Actually, things are very bright," was the opening to a lengthy series of half truths and "best-case scenarios." There was a long and patient silence on the other end of the phone. "Yeah?" he said after some hesitation. "But, are you turning it into cash?" The proverbial jig was up. "Not as well as I should be," was the lame shot at a confession. "Don't worry," he said in a rush to move on to other calls, "you'll be all right. You're still in your stupid stage."

The buzzing of the disconnected line felt like a dentist's drill in my head. What had he meant by "stupid stage," and what did he obviously know that I didn't? These were questions that would nag me for months after his call.

The following Monday started like many others with one notable exception, it marked the week that I would finally get in to see the top guy at a prospective client that I really wanted to work with. He was so difficult to see, due to his travel schedule, that I was a little guarded in my enthusiasm for fear he would cancel and burst my bubble. While I had met him before, I had not done any work for his company in over a year. This was important.

Believe it or not, the day arrived with no canceling message on my trusty answering machine. With the lunch reservations confirmed, I took off to get him. At the restaurant, things went better than I ever could have hoped. We seemed quite compatible and very "in sync" in attitude and disposition. He even went so far as to "apparently self-disclose" some of his thoughts on how my company might strengthen some "soft spots" in his group. All in all, I was feeling great when we reached the door of his building. With the engine running, we sat for a couple of very valuable minutes, during which he expressed a sincere interest in my services. Then he turned and looked me right in the eye and said, "We like what you can do, but we want to see if you are going to make it through your first couple of years in business before we get serious."

"Damn it. What is going on?" was the rhetorical question that burst out three traffic lights from the building. "What am I doing wrong? I just don't get it."

This was clearly not the first time, in the initial 12 months of my company, that I had become frustrated. But it did mark the start of something quite different- ANGER. In the past, I had maintained the capacity to minimize the impact of the pain by labeling it in a more positive fashion, "a learning experience." As a matter of fact, my compulsive tendencies toward note taking after each meeting I had ever attended proved to be invaluable in the "learning from mistakes" mode. Carefully, by design, I had mapped out a "grid" for searching the "techniques landscape," hoping to improve the efficiency of the sales process and enhance the value of my service product. But somehow, nothing was helping. And perhaps the worst part was that I had become introspective and self-critical.

What really bugged me most was that I knew I was a smart person. Master's degree, foreign exchange student, congressional nomination to West Point, and 15 years in the business community. I know my trade. I have sharpened my skills. You'd think, for God's sake, I could figure out what I was doing wrong and fix it, quickly. Yet with all the effort, it was clear that I wasn't making much headway.

Funny thing about anger, it has a way of slipping a black silk bag over your head and neutralizing key senses that would help you solve problems much faster. In my case, I could almost feel the material touch my lips each time I would take a breath. The feeling was like that of drowning.

He called himself a "peddler" by trade. I can still see the tanned, wrinkled skin of his face, and the lines by his eyes looked like they had been made by a bird much heavier than a crow. Hunched over his morning coffee, my retired confidant appeared much more feeble than I ever remembered him. It was at this breakfast chat that I would discover what I had been doing wrong.

After listening patiently to 10 minutes of my whining, he looked up from his poached eggs and smiled. "You know," he said, "you'd be doing great if you were selling your services to yourself. The problem is you're not." "What the hell does that mean," I snapped. "Well," he mused, "you're so all fired quick with the answer that you don't even know the question." More riddles, I thought.

"Didn't you tell me once that you had been a women's shoe salesman?" he asked, seeing that I had completely lost my sense of humor. "Yeah, so what?" was my guarded response. "Well, it has been my experience that buying shoes for a woman has nothing to do with obtaining

95

footwear," he said as he spread orange marmalade on his whole wheat toast. I remember staring at him for an uncomfortably long time struggling to decipher his professorial code. "Think about it for a second," he continued. "Logically, high-heel shoes make no sense at all. They must be terribly uncomfortable, not to mention expensive. So why then does every woman on the planet buy them?" he questioned. "Because of their enhanced self-image when they wear them. That alone should give you the knowledge you need to improve your selling."

The fact that the example was so simple caught me a little flat-footed, and I found myself without retort. As he slid the check across the table, he said, "The best salesman I ever knew sold with his eyes and ears, and not his mouth. Listen 70% and talk 30% and you'll begin to see some results. The reasons people buy things are not always the reasons you think they should." Getting up to leave, he placed his left paw-like hand on my shoulder. The brilliance of his gold Rolex watch seared the credibility of his words into my mind. As he shuffled off, crumpled newspaper under one armpit, I couldn't help smiling with a greater appreciation for the challenge that he had beaten so many years earlier.

That morning, for the price of two breakfast specials and a side order of corned beef hash, I had "learned to be stupid." I had learned that the best mousetrap (or gerbiltrap!), in the world won't sell if the buyer doesn't hate gerbils. And things changed.

Lesson #17

The key to success and profitability in the persuasion process lies in an in-depth understanding of the customers and their needs, not in the sellers and their product.

Chapter Eighteen

Saturday Movies

"I don't want any yes-men around me. I want everybody to tell me the truth even if it costs them their jobs."

– Samuel Goldwyn

The slow, oscillating whir of the fan in the baby's room was the sound that greeted me this morning. Its cool breeze cut the stifling heat, making sleeping less of a chore. Even though the house had central air, the south-facing upstairs bedrooms always needed the fan. Her hair was damp from sweat as I lifted her out of the crib. It was clear from her restlessness that she would not go back to sleep. So this Saturday morning started at 5:15 a.m.

The dogs, too, had not slept very well. As I opened the door to let them out, they lethargically went about their business in a manner uncharacteristic of German Shepards. Struggling to cut through the fog in my head, I managed to change the baby's pants and get the dogs back in the house. Next assignment, breakfast. "Tony flakes," as my daughter calls them, are a sure bet. Add some orange wedges and you're on your way to true infant satisfaction. The dogs were next with their massive "tub" of "large bite" dry mix. A gallon of water to wash it down and you're pretty close.

With the fog lifting slowly, it was time to get the coffee on as quickly as possible. There was tremendous reassurance in the bubbling sound of the automatic drip machine and the accompanying smell that lifts your spirits even though the sun is more than an hour away. Happy grazing sounds were being made by all as the first of the java splashed in

97

the bottom of the cup. As the air conditioner kicked in, things seemed to be going in the right direction.

Once I got all parties cleaned up and things put away, the task became one of keeping everyone busy and quiet until a reasonable hour. The dogs were not a big challenge. With bulging bellies, they slunk off to a corner and flopped down next to an air conditioning duct to resume their slumber. "There is some brilliance there," I thought, as I searched for every "quiet toy" I could find, with the baby clinging to the lapels of my robe. Now if I could barricade us in the family room, I might just have a fighting chance. With the thermos in one hand and the child in the other, I high-stepped the toy box jammed between the couches to the safety of the floor pillows and the TV remote. The room was a disaster of playthings, much to the delight of their master.

The smooth plastic of the remote felt like a "Jedi light saber" on this morning. Finally, some semblance of power and control. With the push of the button, the bright flashing on the screen instilled a sense of confidence that I had been lacking so far. And the mute button saved us all from waking up the master. There is something wonderful about "surfing" through a multitude of obscure cable channels at that hour in the a.m. It is quite bizarre to see the quantity of air time "fillers" that have absolutely no redeeming value whatsoever. But luckily, we had invested in the numerous "pay" channels that, on rare occasion, have something interesting to watch.

Just before completely giving up and being forced to sit through another children's videotape, there it was, the raging open sea, in black and white. Could it be that a movie classic worth viewing would be on this early? Sure enough. For there on the screen, in all of his glory, was Charles Lawton as the notorious "Captain Bligh." And only moments later, appeared Clark Gable as of course, "Fletcher Christian." Having seen the film many times, I have always preferred this version to the one with Marlon Brando.

Ah, the Bounty. What a great movie. But on this particular Saturday morning, I would see something that had escaped me all the times before. As my daughter scribbled wildly in her coloring book, the images on the screen were playing out a scenario in my head which were far too close for coincidence. I "caught up" with the Bounty when she was already at sea. The upbeat marching music was reminiscent of other heroic "swashbuckler" films of the era. The sun, the wind and the billowing sails made you yearn to "press" yourself into service and feel the salt air on your face. Sounds like a certain aftershave commercial, doesn't it. Better still if you whistle.

Soon we came to the part where the crew was on the verge of mutiny and the mighty Bounty had run headlong into a climatic lull. In other words, there was no wind. The listless sails hung limply as the crew tried to stay busy on rationed water. Captain Bligh stood on the bridge and ordered the first of many crews into the life boat to tow the Bounty into a breeze. Shift after shift of rowers whet over the side. The strain on the oars, trying to tow an English vessel of its vintage, must have been unbearable. I remember thinking that the logic for such an act on Captain Bligh's part was quite sound. It would keep the men active and physical while providing a solid objective for motivation. And as the movie plays out, after many tortuous days and nights of effort, the wind did pick up and they were back underway.

But I kept reflecting on the men in the boats, the ones doing the rowing. Here was a situation where, as sailors, they trusted their very lives to something they could not see or predict- the wind. And the irony for me was that when there was no wind, they were willing to go to backbreaking extremes to "find" that which they could not see. They were even willing to leave the relative safety of their ship and brave the possibilities rather than to flounder lifelessly in the ocean.

My wife appeared on the far side of the toy box barricade in her white robe and muffy slippers, looking like I felt. The coffee mug clinched tightly in her hand had my company logo on it, and the sun was finally making an appearance through the window behind her. The squeals of delight from the baby marked the parental "shift change," and for me a second shot at the coffee pot and a shower.

With the steamy water pelting me like a thousand drumming fingers, I couldn't help but think back on what I had just seen. I hadn't sold a job in months. I was angry and frustrated. And worse yet, I had nothing on the horizon. There was no wind. The analogy stuck in my head all through the lathering process, and by the rinse, the rhetorical question had become, "How can I alone tow the business back into the wind?" And, "What kind of a rowboat could I use for towing?" No matter how hard I tried, the towel would not buff the answer into my head.

Sitting at my desk the following Monday morning, I was still puzzling over the questions that had disrupted my weekend. Gazing out over my personal "empire," all 700 square feet of it, I was struck with a sense of my surroundings. There were computers, printers, planning calendars, binders and proposals, all comprising the "ship" of my company. But there was no wind. As the "captain," it was my sworn obligation to search for that which I could not see, yet, upon which I was totally dependent. And for the next three weeks, I did just that.

I painstakingly went through every card in my Rolodex and began making "update" appointments or "just thought we'd have lunch" meetings. Invariably, I would assure the client that I was "unarmed" and "wouldn't try to sell them anything." I just wanted to hear what was on their mind and tell them the latest from our end. This was a method of "leaving the business ship," freeing me to do some personal "towing." Some people reading this book will be going ballistic shouting, "Networking, networking." But I have never been a big believer in time-consuming, generalized networking. Maybe it's a function of the specialized service we provide and a direct result of our business plan. But my "towing" was done on a very calculated course, with a very definite objective in mind.

By the end of that third week, I had been asked for four different proposals, two of which we ended up signing. And by the way, the lessons learned from the "peddler" paid handsome sales dividends in the changes we made to the sales strategies and presentations.

Soon I could feel the cool "salt air" on my face, and in my checkbook. Back on the bridge, it was clear that I had avoided a "mutiny," this time. But the sea, while glorious, can be completely unforgiving.

Splash on the aftershave, guy gets girl, whistle, whistle, whistle. Those ad guys!

Lesson #18

As the captain of "your own ship," you not only have to build it, provide a destination and navigation, but at times even produce the wind for the sails

Chapter Nineteen

AAA Ball

"Baseball is 90% mental, the other half is physical."

– Yogi Berra

And so, the wind blows...now what?

It was late summer and I was on my way home from a sales call on the other side of town. The air conditioning in my 1985 Pontiac was on the fritz, so I was using my 4/55 AC, you know, four windows down at 55 miles per hour. With all the wind noise, I could hardly hear the soft chirping of the car phone. Passers-by found me looking a bit deranged trying to drive, roll up the windows, turn down the radio and talk on the phone all at once. But an incoming call was such a rare treat these days, it was a joy to go through the gyrations.

My ever faithful freelance helper, Mindy, was calling to say that a prospective client had called the office to finally set up the meeting that I had been trying to arrange for the better part of six months. The "smile" in her voice was a wonderful thing to hear, and the news perked up my waning spirits. We exchanged info on the matter, and I was so excited about doing the meeting that I actually had to pull over to dial the number. "Thursday at 10:00 a.m. would be great!" I said, desperately trying to contain myself.

The long drive home that Monday afternoon was one of growing enthusiasm and was even capped off by an impluse stop at a Chinese carryout from a place close to home. I called my wife to say I was bringing dinner. Of course, fried rice for the baby. Even the young, Oriental carryout girl seemed to appreciate my newfound wit. What a country.

Dinner lasted about eight minutes. That's only about one minute shorter than it regularly does with a two-year-old. Eating gear safely stowed in the dishwasher, the rest of the family settled down into the pre-bedtime routine. But my evening's activities had just begun.

My lower level office was abuzz with the sounds of computer hardware startups and the crackling of monitors coming to life. It was time to get busy on the Thursday presentation, right now. All night long, I planned, strategized, cut and pasted my way toward the perfect presentation. As the sun peered over my computer screen that morning, I knew I was well on the way to breaking the "lull" that had haunted me for these many months.

By the end of the day on Tuesday, I was tired and getting a little sloppy in my preparation, so I decided to knock off for the night and catch up on current happenings at the daycare center. The baby had a slight temperature and was somewhat cranky from teething. Mom's nerves were a little frayed from listening to the discontent on the ride home. On this evening, dinner was a chore and not an event. The fatigue and the chaos drove a spike through my forehead that slowly began to choke off rational thinking of any kind. Time for bed.

With Wednesday morning came the first signs of tension and paranoia. Somehow the presentation didn't seem to work as well now as it had late Monday night. I dashed home from the coffee shop and began heavily critiquing the work that I had just spent 48 hours completing. "This is garbage." I thought. It wasn't by the way, but I had lost the ability to control my anxiety. In a cold panic, I began to rip apart the main body of the presentation, fearing that I would look like a fool in front of my new potential client. By lunch, I was a lunatic, charging around, acting as if I was in my "terrible twos." This was my fanny, and I was about to blow it.

Just as I was on the verge of maxing out on the blood pressure chart, the phone rang. It was the new client's secretary. While it is pathetic to say, I only really remember one word of the conversation: "reschedule." You could have amputated my right arm with a rusty, crosscut saw. In deflated silence, I sat there for what seemed to be an hour. When the fog finally cleared, my next emotion was anger. It seems that mister "so and so" was called away on business and wouldn't be available for another TWO WEEKS. I really needed this one, and it wasn't going to happen as planned. That hurt.

Soon, the vision of the irony caught me completely off guard, and I developed a case of the giggles. "What a rookie," I thought. I had been out of practice so long that I had tripped on the top step of the dugout trying to get in the game. That certainly wasn't professional. I couldn't get the vision of me sprawled out on the third baseline with the entire crowd laughing at me, out of my mind. The real kicker was that I had actually done just that in high school, and the imagery still carried the same effect.

So what is the point of even discussing this incident? The point is that there will be times when your abilities as a true professional will be tested. Sure, you will get challenges from the expected places, competitors, rivals, and the like. But this chapter is about learning to deal with the mental conditioning that comes with being a professional, an entrepreneur. Professionalism is an attitude, not to be confused with arrogance. And it is this attitude, cool and confident under pressure, combined with a concoction of skill and luck, that separates those players who eat peanut butter and jelly and ride the bus from those with steak on the team jet.

Lesson #19

True professionals are ready to step into the "batter's box" at a moment's notice and perform brilliantly. Always be prepared for your turn in the "big league."

Chapter Twenty

The Glass Chrysalis

*"Live in such a way that you would not be ashamed
to sell your parrot to the town gossip."*

– Will Rogers

The headline in the Detroit Free Press that morning carried the shocking news about GM's Chairman Bob Stemple and his resignation. If you're in the car business, no matter who you play for, this was a sad day in automotive history. I never had the privilege to meet the man most called "the car guy," but from what I have been told by those who knew him, he was a gem. At first, of course, there was sadness. Not just for Mr. Stemple and his family, but for all of General Motors. The world's largest corporation was bleeding and it was painful to watch.

Once the initial impact of the news wore off, my second reaction was that, given the circumstances, it was probably the right thing to do, change management. Somehow for me the symbolism of events taking place at GM held true to the words, "What is good for GM is good for the country." The country was in the midst of tremendous change, the positives and negatives of which only time will judge.

But the most powerful feeling was unquestionably the sense of paradox that surrounded one man's ascension to one of the most powerful positions in the corporate free world, only to be shattered in one political felled swoop. Here was a man who had worked his whole life to be "king" at his company, and finally got what he had always wanted. In less than two years it would all be over and almost kill him in the process, and arguably, through no fault of his own.

The rustling of newsprint in the next booth snapped me back to reality, and the waitress had arrived just in time with fresh coffee. It was 5:45 a.m. I couldn't help thinking about how many thousands of early morning meetings that Mr. Stemple had attended during his long career at GM. That was all part of the normalization process, the rules of ascension, and he played them, right to the end. He did so because he, as we all do, wanted to get "ahead." Clearly, this means different things to different people. But the point to be made is that Mr. Stemple finally got to the top. For him, there was no more up.

Here is a mind bender. In mathematics they talk about exponential change. This is simply that each successive move changes the situation by at least a multiple of 10. On a purely subjective basis, I would argue that the move from the number two person to the number-one person at a company the size of GM must change things by a minimum of 10 to the third power. While you have all of the power, you also have all of the responsibility. There are two clichés that fit nicely. First, "The buck stops here." And second, "It is lonely at the top."

I would be completely out of my mind to make any direct comparisons between my demure situation and the position that Mr. Stemple was in at GM. But what is worthy of discussion is the applicability of the two clichés to the mindset of the start-up entrepreneur.

Regardless of how you decided to get into business for yourself – either leaving a large company or simply striking out on your own right out of school – one of the most frequently stated reasons for starting a business is "wanting to be your own boss." You could argue that this is representative of a certain personality trait from the beginning. However, there is an adjustment process that takes place over many months and shows up in various ways. For some, it becomes an aggressive, macho "I'm in charge," complex that has its pluses and minuses. In others, it is the compulsive caretaker attitude, and this is the person who is always at work, both mentally and physically.

While I tend toward the compulsive side of the spectrum, what I am hoping to convey in this chapter is what I have come to call "mental cocooning." From the label, you already begin to conjure up images. What I don't want you to do is walk away with the idea that this is a recommended trait. It is something that happens that you must watch for carefully.

It was November of our first full calendar year, and even though the icy winter winds whipped down the cul de sac, we were sweating bullets that this Christmas would be less than lean. The figures told us that we were having a solid first year, but with the initial start-up costs and computer hardware, we wouldn't be vacationing in Jamaica for a while. With six weeks to go, and no job on the plate, the chances of bumping up the year-end numbers were slim.

The call came in a little after 2:00 p.m. on Friday the 20th. The voice on the phone was that of an old agency buddy who had left to work for a Chrysler agency. We had been trying to push through an assignment with his new firm for over a year. After months of persistence, and some outstanding inside selling on his part, our shot had finally arrived. "We're approved, let's rock and roll," was the verbal green light I had waited so long to hear. I had never "high-fived" myself before, but with this victory, I felt compelled to try.

Recalling the lessons learned in my bout with "semipro status" (AAA Ball), this project was going to be a model of a focused, efficient and high-quality effort. The rest of that afternoon was spent on building the contracts and setting up the working files. After a quick soak in the hot tub and a shot of sweet sherry, I hit the bed early to get a good night's sleep. On Monday morning, we were going to hit it real hard.

The weekend seemed to drag by. I found myself drifting in and out of daydreams. Finally, my wife asked me point blank why I was being so distant. Nothing on television interested me. And only the daily routine kept me away from the computer keyboard. I felt like a thoroughbred just before entering the gate.

Monday arrived, as it traditionally does, with one big exception: this one was to be the beginning of a mission. For the next 14 days, I was a man possessed. Eighteen-hour days were the norm, and I even posted two 24 hour marathons. On the 11th of December 1992, I handed over the finished product. It was exactly what I wanted. Solid. On time and on budget. The client was extremely pleased.

But this section is not about stamina or maintaining focus. These are items that are expected. Rather, it is about the effect this type of behavior has on others and your reaction to them. I knew in my heart, that it was of the utmost importance that this be done right, no compromises.

It would take more than 100% effort, and I was willing to go the extra mile. But for a little over two weeks, nothing- and I mean nothing- else mattered. My daughter, who is an angel, became a nuisance. My wife simply didn't exist. No personal phone calls were returned. Bills didn't get paid. Life just stopped.

Here is the irony. When confronted about this behavior, I was furious. "Why won't these people just leave me alone? Can't they see I have a business to run?" were typical under-my-breath retorts. People around me felt that I had become untouchable, and I kept driving the disciplined focus inward, hoping that it would all result in a metamorphosis. I desperately needed the feeling of security in the decisions that were being made, and I actually ended up sleeping in a sleeping bag on the couch for the tactile comfort.

Does this all sound bizarre? Well, here is the point. Earlier I said that Mr. Stemple had gotten what he wanted, the top job and there was no up. Suddenly he found himself surrounded by people, but completely alone. As a start-up entrepreneur, you, too, will be alone. There is no up and, in some cases, no down either. You will find yourself completely surrounded at times, yet totally on your own. A great deal is at stake each time you ship a job. With competition as keen as it is, the product must be right all the time. There will be great pressure on you to perform consistently. You will feel obligated to go into the "cocoon," but this will only be tolerated by those around you if it produces a butterfly.

The truth is that it would be much easier to do if you could hide during the effort. But unfortunately, this is a glass chrysalis, and everyone is watching.

Lesson #20

While it will distress you beyond comprehension, do not be surprised when those around you do not share the same sense of urgency over a situation that you created. Don't go into a shell. Walls that protect also confine. Always remember, you wanted to be "in charge," and now you are.

Chapter Twenty-One

Flatlining

"When you arrive at your future, will you blame your past?"

– Robert Half

To say the least, having your own business is one of the most dynamic emotional roller coasters you will ever ride on. The good times will rocket you skyward with heart-pounding glee. The not-so-good times will plummet you back to earth while wrenching your guts out and leaving your heart in your throat. But one thing is for sure, you paid your money knowing full well what to expect. Right?

Everyone loves a good theme park. In the corporate world, I knew a lot of people who got lost in Fantasy Land. These were the folks who completely avoided the dangerous rides and, instead, indulged their every whim on corporate expense account money. I often referred to them as "Walters," as in Walter Mitty. As American business continues to restructure, these folks are going to find Fantasy Land closed for remodeling.

When you decide to hang out your own shingle, you're in for some mental remodeling of your own. Most of it you will implement yourself. Some of it will come crashing down on top of you. In either case, change is not only probable, but imminent.

I have talked a great deal about change so far, both positive and negative. Yet in writing this chapter, I feel more compelled than in any other to clearly articulate a condition that, if not properly dealt with, can have devastating effects. As the title of this section indicates, I call it "flatlining."

If you have stayed with me to this point, you have no doubt vicariously experienced the same roller coaster I have been on since the beginning. And what a ride it has been. Even now, I am still not completely weaned off the motion sickness medication required to get me through another fiscal quarter. This, figuratively speaking of course. However, I have found that as time goes on, the dosage gets smaller and smaller.

Imagine what it would be like to lose your fear of the roller coaster, or the thrill of exhilaration, completely. Let's face it, your mental and physical response systems are in place to protect you from great bodily harm. These are the same ones that let you enjoy the experience. But what if, whether voluntarily or involuntarily, knowingly or unknowingly, these response systems were turned off and kept off over an extended period of time? Can you imagine the possible outcomes? If this sounds like so much conceptual double talk, please stay with me while I explain the point.

On a frigid January, the postal lady delivered the second largest check I had ever received in my life. Words are incapable of describing the feeling of holding a large check between two sets of pinched fingers. This was not corporate monopoly money, this was mine – OK, and the IRS's. With one stroke of a pen, I had more money in a bank account than in all the cumulative years of trying to that point. But for me, the jubilation was more than the dollar figure. It was about the realization that a genuinely better life was, in fact, possible. All along, I had always wanted to believe it. That day, I did.

The roller coaster felt more like the space shuttle. And I was clearly in orbit. By the way, financial "weightlessness," even if temporary, is wonderful.

Reentry was a little hotter than I expected. Somewhere in the checks for the tax man, business insurance, auto repair, computer hardware, accounting and legal fees, etc. came the crashing realization that I "wasn't in Kansas anymore, Toto." It seemed that my dreams were being doled out like so much birdseed to hungry vultures. Start-up costs had become a monetary hemorrhage, and I was without a tourniquet.

Now the roller coaster had corkscrewed me into the asphalt, and I walked around in a state of shock for about two weeks. Had it not been for some financial footwork, we may have had to turn the lights out early in the going.

I can go on and on with examples like this, but the point is that during this ride, something inside began to change. Defense mechanisms began to take over and at first, I intentionally would not allow myself to go up as high when things went well, or down as low when they didn't. My life had become a "sign" curve, and I was deliberately chopping off the peaks and valleys. Over time, the range of emotional flexibility narrowed considerably.

Let me give you some idea of the ways this presents itself. Conversations would take place like, "Steve, we just got the X project," "Great" I would say. "Now, this is going to be a lot of work, so this is how we are going to tackle it." Or, "Steve, we didn't get the job on the Z program." "Fine, what we need is a proposal on the C job and we'll need it tomorrow," was a typical response. Do you begin to get the picture? There was no good or bad, just a driven tunnel vision to move forward, wherever that was.

Maybe you've heard the phrase, "If you get hurt in business, you shouldn't be in it." Well, while there is a degree of truth to this, I would argue that if you don't care enough to get emotionally involved to some extent, you have motivational cards you're not showing. "Trust" just took a rocket ride to the basement.

It is critical that you become aware and closely monitor this narrowing range of emotional flexibility. I believe, though I have not experienced it directly, that you will reach a point at which the progression becomes involuntary and you run the risk of falling into deep depression. Remember, you are not running this business in a vacuum. Others around you only increase the pressure, and you will find yourself reacting to their ups and downs in much the same manner.

Why does this idea of emotionally "flatlining" bother me so much? First of all, you went into business to enjoy the roller coaster ride, the ups and downs, the competitive battle of it all. Remember what I said earlier? If you jumped in for the money only, you're in deep and treacherous water. Second, everyone reacts to pressure differently. I will argue to you that this narrow range of flexibility contributes to the high percentage of divorce, alcoholism, drug use and worse. Third, clinical depression is not to be taken lightly. And finally, while you will be convinced otherwise, you are no longer in control of yourself or your company. It's hard enough when you have a full array of senses to draw upon, let alone to fight the wars emotionally handcuffed.

Discipline and focus are two critical elements in any successful business. I believe in them and practice each to the best of my ability. What I am referring to here, in the notion of "flatlining," is a loss of perspective. This loss will undermine every aspect of the decision-making process. It represents a very false sense of security. New entrepreneurs, trying too desperately to succeed, are much more apt to fall into this than the crafty veteran who has bigger numbers on the experience odometer.

The movie "Stripes" had a wonderful line in it delivered by the drill sergeant to a new recruit self nicknamed, "Psycho." Whenever the recruit would say, "Touch my stuff, I kill ya," the Sarge would respond, "Lighten up, Francis."

Lesson #21

Don't fool yourself into thinking that you can become a "business machine" and factor out emotion as a method of reducing stress. It limits your perspective and actually increases your internal stress load.

Chapter Twenty-Two

The Better Half

*"The meeting of two personalities is like
the contact of two chemical substances:
if there is any reaction, both are transformed."*

– Carl Jung

I'll bet you're hoping that I am going to talk about an upturn in the last two quarters of the fiscal year. If only it were that simple! This is a discussion of when your single biggest asset becomes a major liability, or so you think.

"You don't seem to smile as much as you used to," I remember my mother saying to me over coffee one morning. "Is something wrong at home?" "Of course not," was my well-rehearsed response. "Things are fine, and I know what to do," I quietly reassured her.

But there was a tremendous turmoil in my head and heart that was carefully walking the fine line between confusion and outright panic. Subtly, somehow imperceptibly, things had changed.

As I sit here scanning the recesses of my brain for a place to start, groping for explanations and maybe even apologies, I can't seem to escape the pressing sense of isolation. If you were to ask my spouse to this instant how things were in our relationship, I am willing to bet she would use words like "fine, normal and same as always, though a lot more tense." The analysts out there will quickly say, "She doesn't have a problem, you do." Which brings me to the topic of this section, namely, The problem you will have with yourself, about your spouse."

Realizing that I am constrained by the singular male perspective, I will do my best to be generic on the issues so as not to bear the potential wrath of my female readers. Trust me, the issues are big enough to be easily translatable. Here goes.

Having or starting a new business when you are married demands a commitment by both parties. Don't let anyone tell you differently. The easiest analogy I can give you is like when you get your first puppy. Clearly, a joint decision. What a joyous event. You both want to hug him and pet his ears. For a while, you're even willing to take him in the car and do silly things like buy him yogurt at the local strip mall. But then the housebreaking begins, and the trips to the vet, and the traditional destruction of expensive shoes. Sooner or later, here it comes. Those inevitable words that divide you like a cheap cubical. The time your spouse announces in no uncertain terms that YOUR dog has just relieved himself on the living room carpet, and YOU had better get your fat butt off the sofa and clean up YOUR mess!" Sound vaguely familiar? In the worst-case scenario, you can always get rid of the dog. That's why I didn't choose a child for the analogy. Of course, you can always choose to shut down the business if things get too ugly. The difference will be in the net effect of the move.

Wait a second. What has happened here? There are several subtleties that need to be aired and discussed. First, the decision to buy the dog in the first place, may or may not be as joint a decision as you thought. By the outcome, it was evidently not her first choice and was probably a tolerance of your wishes, at least that is how they will see it.

I distinctly remember the day when I decided to "go for it" and start my own company. On the one hand, there was tremendous relief from the gut-wrenching agony leading up to the decision. On the other hand, there was foresight into the rocky and winding road that lay ahead. My wife has always been supportive of me and my nature. But with the possibility of the financial downside that loomed ominously on the horizon, simple support would not nearly cover the trials and tribulations that waited. It was going to take a commitment on her part as well, one that might set back our combined lifestyles by many years. This was not to be taken lightly.

Even though I consider myself to be a fair salesperson, here is the essence of the presentation you are trying to make to your spouse. "Dear, I would like to risk the house, cars and our entire family's financial future on the possibility that I can make a business that I have never tried professionally, successfully. Hon, trust me." Folks, if you think that is an easy pitch, you're kidding yourself.

The second issue is the motivation for wanting to start the business. We know why we want our own company, the fulfillment of a dream, right? But whose dream is it? Remember, it is yours and not your spouses. This is a fact that you may be reminded of the second time you can't make the mortgage payment. It is important to keep in mind that a certain degree of skepticism by your spouse is good. This tells me that they understand the degree of difficulty. Beware of a mate that quickly agrees with giggling enthusiasm. They may be laughing at you when the judge gives them the house, too.

A third issue has to do with the degree of risk-taking your spouse has displayed in the past. But, a word of caution. Things change as your stage in life changes. If you suddenly decide to bolt from your company after 17 years, with two kids approaching college and a mortgage payment that took three tries to get approved, don't expect your spouse to get excited about upsetting the apple cart. This is not the same carefree, live-for-today person you married years ago. Tolerance levels for your "larks" have changed significantly.

Finally, and most importantly, you will be completely oblivious to everything I have said so far. If you have gotten to the leveraged stage of seriously considering the jump, be careful. You have already lost most of your ability to objectively discuss your spouse's attitudes and feelings. Be prepared for the anger that you will express if they show any reservations toward the move. "My God, this is my one big shot," and "Why can't you understand that this is important to me," and "I have busted my butt for years to build a better life for this family and now you're giving me crap." Get the picture?

Worse, now you have armed them with a four-word nuclear arsenal for when things hit bottom: "I told you so." And the strange thing about this is that you have done this to yourself. But again, you will develop a selective memory about this.

While it may seem that I am only talking to the married people out there, you can see how the same issues would apply to "significant others" as well. Businesses take time and nurturing. There is a finite amount of both available. A spouse is going to need to be more than tolerant, they are going to have to genuinely approve and get involved emotionally. I have the belief that while you can share events in life, you really can't share emotions. It is unrealistic to think you can.

I have described the isolation of being a startup entrepreneur. And I have even attempted to demonstrate how to use this isolation as a positive before it unknowingly becomes a negative. But what is very difficult to articulate is the invisible tether that a spouse can provide that can keep you from going over the edge and slipping into depression. The spouse, on the other hand, needs to let the entrepreneur "have enough slack" so as not to hang themselves, yet gives them the security to know that there is a supporter when things go awry.

The job of the spouse is perhaps more difficult in some ways. Each day and each successive phase will create its share of challenges. The thing to realize is that the whole experience will permanently affect those involved. I have heard the spouses of several business friends say that they felt that their lives had to go on hold while the business grew. To them I can only say that, while I understand their position completely, entrepreneurialism is a lifestyle unto itself. You either work with that and enjoy it, or you both must decide that it is not right for your mutual happiness. These things must be discussed. The challenge is, they often are overlooked in the heat of battle.

My wife and I have two German shepherds. When they were pups, we loved them to a fault, but they were both a major pain in the butt. Over time, we had to learn to live with them and they with us. And even though they still make me crazy at times, they have brought us great joy.

You might say I'm still paper training my business. By the way, my wife still helps me pick up the yard.

Lesson #22

You must be sure to involve your spouse or significant other in the decision to move forward with a business. They must be "on board" emotionally, or the added stress will be very difficult to shoulder. Remember, this is your dream, not theirs.

Chapter Twenty-Three

Work Toward Lincoln, But Take the Washingtons

"The most beautiful words in the English language are 'Check Enclosed.'"

– Dorothy Parker

In 1966, at the age of 10, I was persuaded to join a neighborhood "rock band" made up of other 10 year olds from the nearby elementary school. While we were very young and inexperienced, we practiced religiously in a garage up the block. At first, we didn't have very much equipment. To be sure, we were "unplugged," not due to a particular artistic vision, but rather a distinct lack of funds.

As I recall, it was our lead guitarist, whose parents were the most well off, that received the first electric instrument along with a significantly powerful amplifier for the day. Next, the keyboard player moved to "high voltage." The drummer ended up with most of this gear as a "Santa surprise" that Christmas. That left me.

My folks shopped around in the newspaper for my electric guitar and finally found a used instrument that was in excellent condition. It was not a name brand, but it didn't matter. This was my ticket to the glamour and money of big-time rock and roll. There was only one problem, no amplifier. For a while, the other guitar player let me plug into his gear. Soon, it was clear that I needed my own stuff since the band was growing and becoming more demanding.

During a trip to a local Kmart store with my mother, I happened to spot a "beginner" amplifier in one of the departments. With wide-eyed enthusiasm, I checked it out and decided this was exactly what I needed. The only real challenge was the price, $50. Needless to say, at 10 I didn't have that kind of money lying around. When I confronted my parents, they astutely recommended that I find a way to earn the money for the object of my desire. But how?

It was early spring of 1967 when my dad approached me about the possibility of cutting the neighbor's lawn as a method of generating the cash. So with great apprehension, I shuffled up to the door and looked into the opportunity. To my utter amazement, he loved the idea and we agreed on a financial arrangement, $4 per cut, once a week. If you do the math on this situation, you will discover that I had just signed up for a 13-week project, at minimum, if I was to have the necessary money for my amp.

Week after week I cut the grass, and week after week I got my $4. It was actually quite wonderful to watch the money pile up in my cigar box as time went along. By the first week of September, I had the money to make my purchase. I was very proud and so were my folks. Mom took me up to Kmart that Saturday, and we charged down the aisles with unbridled excitement. And there it was, with only one small difficulty. Over the summer, the store had raised the price to $63. Even at 11-years-old, I was unable to fight back the tears. Mom, too, felt my heart-wrenching let down and chipped in the money to make up the difference. We walked out of the store that day with a new amplifier and a new closeness in our relationship.

As you have gathered by now, this section is about the money. I almost titled this chapter, "A frank discussion about money," but that seemed much too lecture-oriented and would not capture the essence of what really needs to be said. Please give me some latitude here and I won't sound too preachy.

Some people are simply better with money than others. Handling money is not an innate skill, it must be learned. Having said that, everyone should be able to achieve some level of skill if they so desire. But I have run into so many people who think with their egos instead of their heads, that are successful, that there must be something to it beyond what you learn in a classroom.

I believe that one of the biggest keys to the successful handling of dollars for the startup entrepreneur is "attitude." Money, in a small business, is simply the lubricant that keeps the wheels turning. Cost control and cash flow are critical elements to watch if you are going to carefully monitor the "pulse" of your organization. As I have said earlier, I have a tendency to be somewhat compulsive from an organizational standpoint. We have all the standard monthly cost accounting sheets and financial projections, all based, however, on building the company according to our business plan. Here is where the attitude part comes in. If you can maintain a longer-term perspective, even though the wolf may be at the door, you stand a better chance of making it over the long haul. Conversely, I have seen people run out and buy the big car once they got that first large check, and go under six months later.

You're probably saying to yourself, what's the big deal? I learned all that as a teenager. The point is that learning to cope with the insecurity of not receiving a paycheck on the 15th and 30th can bend your head if you let it. It is easy to err on the side of ultra-conservatism and save your way into extinction. As an example, you must promote your business to increase business, but promotion is expensive. So, you may decide to cut back or stop promoting altogether. You shouldn't be surprised when the business doesn't materialize. This is just one of many "catch 22s" you will encounter.

The next biggest key is in the way you prepare to handle your taxes. One day when I was complaining to a buddy about a large tax check I had just written, he said, "Hey, if you don't pay taxes, you didn't make any money." That thinking rearranged my attitude toward the IRS. Speaking of them, there is a lot of comfort in knowing that you are totally prepared for an audit should it occur. Don't be lax on the bookkeeping of the business or you will find yourself at the end of the year in one hell of a mess with no place to hide. You don't need an ulcer at Christmas.

The last thing I want to talk about also has to do with your attitude, and that is, how you price your goods and services. Price positioning strategies are the subject of every marketing textbook worth its salt. I highly advise looking into these when you are writing your business plan. But, my point is to be made in a slightly different vein.

When I left to start my own company, whether I was able to admit it or not, I had an ax to grind. I was going to make up for all the lost time and money I felt the old company owed me. In other words, I felt that my services were worth more than reality would prove. By pricing my services too high for the demand in the market, I essentially pigeonholed myself and didn't get the start I was looking for. On the other hand, however, by under pricing the product just to get the business, or being willing to operate at a net loss, is a formula for disaster as well. What I am trying to say is that the marketplace should determine the proper price points as compared to cost to give you the best chance of maximizing the business and profit. Give up on trying to get even.

The first several years will be a financial learning experience based on survival. While we all want to do great things, reality will dictate a more patient approach. Wanda the waitress said something one day on this subject I felt was quite appropriate. Trying my best to be amusing, I asked her if she would accept a torn one-dollar bill. She smiled at me and said, "Young man, a small basket of torn ones paid for that Chevy in the parking lot, but I'd be walking if I tried to buy gas with the fives that people give away." Point well taken.

Lesson #23

There is a tremendous difference between earning money and managing money. Most people are good at one or the other. In the early phases of your business, the only real objective for making and managing money should be continued growth.

Chapter Twenty-Four

Banker Bondage

"A lot of people will urge you to put some money in a bank. But don't go overboard. Remember, businessmen who run banks are so worried about holding on to things that they put little chains on all their pens."

– Miss Piggy

I hate cubicles, especially in a bank. While they present the facade of privacy, they are nothing more than "inhibition reducers" that encourage you to say things in public that might otherwise be better left unsaid. This day's drive to the bank was done with more than mild trepidation, because I knew that it was going to be far more than an ATM transaction. A cubical was about to serve as a confessional.

For reasons still unknown to me, I had decided to wear a necktie and a double- breasted suit to handle this meeting. Perhaps the appearance of success would hold some merit. This is the same logic that felons use in court with the judge. In my heart, I knew that it would have little or no positive effect. Turning off the ignition key, safely tucked into a close-up parking slot, I took a deep breath and prepared to have a meeting that had wrenched my guts for several weeks. With no more places to hide, I walked as briskly and confidently as I could through the front door and into the waiting area.

The reason for the meeting was quite clear. I was out of money. Not kind of, but flat broke. In all of our combined checking and savings accounts, we had less than $600. The worst part was that I had $2000 worth of bills due in four days and, obviously, the two ends were not about to meet. In anticipation of this situation and this day, I had been physically ill for several weeks. Now there was no place to hide and I needed help, big time.

Of all the people you know, I'll bet I have one of the best credit ratings of anybody. Hell, I even paid off my student loan two years early! I hate debt. To me, it had always represented a sign of weakness and a lack of discipline. But there I was, for the first time in my life, and it was a loathsome, hateful experience I will forever strive to avoid. The internal humiliation of sitting in that carpeted area at the bank brought with it a paranoia that everyone knew why I was there. And to make matters worse, I was going to have to describe my pain in a cubical.

After several long minutes of fidgeting in the chair, an attractive, professionally dressed woman in her mid 40s motioned to me and asked how she could be of help. With the ceremonial handshake behind us, I sat down and began reciting a carefully worded speech about the need for a short-term business loan, payable immediately. Her body language quickly informed me that I might as well have been presenting to the IRS and that there was no way she was going to come up with any bank money for my cause. Reading the rosiness of my cheek and the panic in my eyes, she politely allowed me to finish and kindly figured a way for me to save face in this situation.

When I was done, she leaned back and asked how many years of company bank statements I could show. "One," was the only answer I could provide. "Well, you would need at least three," she calmly responded. After a few minutes of digging around on her desk and accessing my records on her computer screen, the best advice she could muster was for me to apply for the bank's revolving line of credit. In other words, we can't help you. With my heart sinking, and on the verge of panic, my eyes began to swell with tears and I literally begged her to find a way to get me $2,500 immediately. After searching my personal credit cards, she managed to accumulate a cash advance for the money I needed. The walk out of the bank and to my car was like every eye in the place was on me, and they were all laughing. Never have I felt so financially small, and alone.

When I was with the ad agency, and my wife was with her old firm, we had never even considered the notion of being turned down for a loan, of any amount. To this point in my life, the ability to borrow was only limited by my desire to spend. Cars, no problem. Houses, no sweat. But right this minute I needed a relatively small amount of money, and was nearly turned down flat. This was a brand new and less-than-flattering experience.

By the way, I did manage to survive the toughest month in my company's young history. What I have not told you is that I had a receivable that was overdue when all of this chaos was going on. So I knew that the money was on its way, but not in hand. The transitional nature of this situation broke the experience to me in a very gentle form, in retrospect. However, I will never again have to be shot to know that it hurts.

What is the point of even bringing this up as a topic or as a separate section? This book is about learning to deal with yourself and the changes you will encounter. Never before had I considered how difficult it would be to borrow money when I needed it. And why should I? It had never been a problem in the past. I'll bet many of you are in the same boat. Trust me when I tell you that somewhere in your first several years of operation, unless you are incredibly lucky, you will need to borrow. The only way that will happen is if you have pre-established a relationship with a bank to allow for a small signature line of credit well in advance of starting your own company. Once you are on the outside, you will have lost a golden opportunity to save yourself a great deal of pain and aggravation. Get to know a banker on a first-name basis right now. Don't find yourself sitting in a cubical confessing your problems to an uninterested branch manager in your hour of need.

I genuinely want to believe that each experience makes you stronger in the long run. The lessons learned in this saga, while not guaranteeing their lack of recurring, served as a reality reminder that things have changed in my life, and that business as usual was no longer going to work. It was unfortunate that I had to become financially handcuffed to find this out. While it hurt to have to grovel for the money to carry on, an indirect benefit was the increase in motivation that came from it. In another chapter, I said that "fear either mobilizes or paralyzes," and in this case I was off to the races that following Monday morning.

Lesson #24

Establish your cash credit lines while you are still employed by your current firm. Once you have to list "self-employed" on a credit application, your chances of being approved in the first several years are substantially reduced.

Chapter Twenty-Five

Body Surfing

*"Success is going from failure to failure
without losing your enthusiasm."*

– Sir Winston Churchill

In the last section I mentioned the IRS. Well, I have a suggestion for them as it relates to entrepreneurs. Vacations should be a tax deductible item placed under "medical expenses." Since striking out on my own, the few getaways I did manage came at a time when my wife and I were on the verge of collapse. We would both spend the first four days, of seven, in the room sleeping and being physically ill. The last three days were spent mustering the energy to pack for the trip home. This was not exactly my idea of fun in the sun.

I'll bet it's psychosomatic, but I have a tendency to "get well" faster if I spend some time in and around salt water. Suntanned, well-oiled hard bodies don't hurt either, but that's a different story altogether. One of my favorite activities is to mindlessly bob up and down in the rolling surf, often balancing a frozen margarita. There is something about the energy of the waves and that semi-weightless feeling that is a real tension reliever. After scanning the horizon for several minutes, I like to make a fool of myself by swimming like crazy to catch the perfect wave for some great body surfing. The rush of the water and the sudden surge of power is great fun for the short time it lasts.

This chapter is about learning how to body surf the "swells" of business that you will encounter. It is also about recognizing the difference between a good wave to ride and the one you bob over.

While at times you may doubt whether or not it will really happen, business will pick up. In our first year we had just finished a nice project before Christmas, and projections for the first quarter of the next year looked promising. There were a lot of proposals on people's desks around town, and talk of approval was beginning to creep into conversations. After sizing up the potential workload and matching them against resources, it became obvious that we would need upgraded computer gear to get everything handled. The conservatism in my capital expenditures nature cautioned me against rash purchase decisions without signed contracts. So we waited.

By the 20th of January, it was obvious that things were not going to pan out as cleanly as originally planned. One by one, we got the traditional, "Due to budget constraints... and, the timing is just not right..." lines that change the status sheet from "pending" to "killed." As the projected receivables failed to arrive, we were real glad that we didn't rush out and upgrade our systems. This was just a "swell," and not a rideable wave.

Time passed, and we mustered another barrage of proposals based on a new sales strategy. We were able to sign one deal in the office the day of the presentation and had two others on "very favorable" status. With a signed contract in hand, we bought the gear we needed, and only what we needed, to get through the next quarter. As luck would have it, we were able to sign the other two and end up with a great couple of months.

There are several points to be made in contrasting these incidents. First, we had learned from experience that picking the right time to act, or wave to ride, is as much an art as it is a science. You must develop the ability to read your clients and build a relationship that allows them to be candid up front on the possibility of securing the business. Don't assume anything. If you select a wave that is too large with risk and downside expense burdens, you might well be crushed under its weight.

Second, you must be prepared when the opportunity is right. When things are slow, we spend a great deal of time and energy training on computers, redoing the files, updating mailing lists, making sure the accounting is current, etc. The outside casual observer might consider this busy work. If these things were done without a specific purpose, they might be right. However, we hustle to stay current so that when we get the assignment, we are ready to act on a moment's notice with all guns blazing. When I worked as a supervisor at United Parcel Service, we had a saying that really capsulized operating efficiency and it was, "Clean up starts at the beginning of the day."

Third, upturns in business are dynamic by nature. In other words, they are not going to wait for you. Often, and I might even say in all cases, you are going to have to "paddle like crazy" to catch up with them to harness their power. I have seen several of my friends literally miss the bus on major opportunities because they didn't get a running start. If you have ever missed a wave, you know the feeling of standing there, wet and bewildered, watching others having a great time at your expense.

Fourth, when things do start to surge, it is critical to maintain your sense of balance. My nature is to chase things down all at once and stay way out in front of the project, or surge. But I have learned that there are inevitable changes in direction and tempo. If you are off balance and too far forward, you will have wasted your time and efforts trying to over-anticipate what will happen. You must stay current, flexible and, above all, balanced in your approach.

Finally, you must learn when to get out. This was a lesson I got when I tried to milk an upturn too long and found that I had, instead, missed the next major surge because I was playing with trivialities and was not ready. The feeling was like having wet hair in your face and sand in your pants. All you could do was slog your way back into the pounding surf. When I talk about "getting out," I do not mean abandoning work in progress or failing to follow up on closing details. These are critical things to do to maintain your professionalism and credibility. What I am referring to is allowing yourself to be taken advantage of in the hopes that more business will come of it. It usually doesn't.

To close this section, I will remind you that all business surges, like waves or swells, have a beginning and an end. This knowledge allows you to measure them over time to better understand their dynamics and how to deal with them. One of the biggest challenges all business seems to have from a cost overhead standpoint is that people always want to staff and be ready for the "peaks" of the surge, and must live with the expense burden when it is over. Conversely, you can be too lean and unprepared for the upturn and get crushed by it. My advice in learning to "body surf" the business surges is to fully understand your capabilities and be ready for the median of the cycle. When things get busy, dig in and work more hours, hire freelancers or temporary help, etc. But don't be tempted to add overhead until the level of the ocean itself rises.

As I dug my toes into the sand on the beach in Ponce Inlet, Florida, I remember the noon sun baking down on my pale white back. Watching the waves roll in and feeling like I had just been hit by a bus, I couldn't help but think, "I wouldn't be here now, enjoying this vacation, if the clients hadn't been so kind in beating me to death with their trust in my company." This Bud's for me!

Lesson #25

Business cycles must be managed and overhead controlled. If you plan your operating levels for maximum output levels and the business doesn't materialize, you will be in major trouble. It is far easier to expand than it is to cut back.

Chapter Twenty-Six

The Apple Principle

"I'm thirty-years old, but I read at the thirty-four-year-old level."

– Dana Carvey

In September of 1980, after an extended time away from college, I made the decision to return to school and finish up at Michigan State. At 24, I was one of the oldest juniors in most of the classes, a fact that embarrassed me. The years leading up to my return were filled with all the exploits you might imagine a young male making a decent wage would be involved in. Carefree, and in no particular hurry, time was a friend to be frivolous with. But through some rather fateful circumstances, life seemed to provide a much-needed wake-up call. In retrospect, I had come to a fork in the road. The choice of which path to take would be both the best and the most difficult of my life.

The first day of orientation, I had to fill out a form declaring a major. A check mark next to "undecided" automatically herded me into a room with other less-insightful fellow students. With the last name of Brown, I was near the top of the list to chat with the guidance counselors. After a half-hour of inarticulate musing on my part, the two counselors nodded at each other and simultaneously said, "Communications." To this day I am convinced that this must be the frustration pile for the counselors. But, the die had been cast.

There were, however, two things I was able to tell them with complete confidence: how long I was going to be at Michigan State, and what I was going to accomplish. I had spent the time figuring out what it was costing me, on a daily basis, to be at school. This was based on lost wages, housing costs, tuition, etc. The other thing was, I was paying for this adventure. No free meal ticket here. So, I had decided that I could only afford to be there twenty four months, max. When it came to the goal, that was clear, Master's Degree. Nothing else would do. The bottom line to this discussion was that I had told the counselor that I was going to get my junior and senior years finished, and complete the Master's program, all in two years. Politely, they both smiled and said it couldn't be done.

I had set a goal for myself, and I was determined to reach it. But I had no idea of the mental and physical demands required to get it done. For two years, seven days a week, 16 hours a day, I pressed the limits of my abilities and resources to the very brink of complete collapse. In several chapters, I have talked about the "edge." What I am referring to is the capacity to carry on physically, while maintaining the will to do so mentally.

Why have I bothered telling you this? And more importantly, why should it matter to you? There are many stories of unheralded survival in situations imposed upon people. You could rattle off a list including storm victims, accident survivors, and the like. These are all situations that tax the human spirit in a variety of ways. Yet, they have one element in common- that is the imposed or passive structure that established the challenge. Stepping up to the challenge in these situations was a response to a formidable stimulus. On a more obscure level, one might argue that climbing the corporate ladder, or swimming with the corporate sharks, as it were, is based on the same imposed situation. Many would consider it fighting for their very lives.

My college experience, as described above, is one example of an unimposed structure; in other words, one that you have built yourself. The courage and bravery of people in imposed situations is genuinely inspiring to me. It serves to prove what we are capable of if properly motivated. But what is even more impressive is what some people can accomplish with the power of a highly motivated and determined will. Stories of people losing weight and changing their lives, mountain climbers conquering that impenetrable peak, astronauts walking on the moon, marathon runners, all stir my imagination because these folks chose to undertake these things of their own free will.

I am not a clinical psychiatrist. But I would argue that the art of driving your body and mind beyond what might be reasonably expected, or considered normal, by choice, is a different kettle of fish completely. Professional athletes are perhaps the most visible example of people who have made a science out of preparing for the combined challenges of their chosen career. Health, both physical and mental, is their number-one priority, and the sole reason they are in the position they're in. The long, hard hours of training, in a gym where there are no cheering fans or adoring well wishers, is the difference between success and failure.

Why should this be important to you? Having been through the college experience, I had some idea of what to expect when striking out on my own. About a year before leaving my old company, I started getting my physical act together. Stretching and bending exercises were the precursor to more exhaustive jogging. I even went out and bought one of those cross-country skiing machines and a stair stepper. The stamina required to tackle the first couple of years in business, long hours and seven days a week, will beat you into submission and exhaustion if you don't prepare for it. I find that the worst mistakes I have made so far are fatigue errors 99% of the time. You will not be able to operate effectively if you are tired and weak, so don't be. This is something that can be controlled if you step up to the training in advance.

The physical part might be the easy part. Training what goes on inside your head is often much more difficult. Experts would argue that pressure and stress are a function of relative perspective. When I was with the ad agency, decisions made regarding millions of dollars of company money were a lot less stressful than those made with $100 in my corporate account and a drawer full of bills. Your own business, while smaller in scope to things you may be used to, will place demands on your ability to maintain your composure far beyond your wildest comprehension. Stress-level tolerance will be tested and re-tested, almost on a daily basis.

But how does one go about training the mind for the entrepreneurial journey ahead? In my view, it is critical that you revive the ability to accomplish established goals outside your current working environment. Let me give you a couple of examples. How are you doing on the diet you started six months ago? Have you stained the deck like you told your neighbor? What about that first flying lesson you promised yourself? These are all small, doable things that you can't seem to find time for, right? Get them done. My suggestion for you is to get back in the driver's seat of setting and accomplishing goals in a timely fashion. You will find that the exercise is not only satisfying, it's contagious.

Next, turn off your television and get used to it being off. As an entrepreneur, you won't have much use or time for it. In the ad business, we had a shop phrase for people like me, "light TV viewer." The reality of it, however, is more like, "unbelievably light TV viewer." With all of the elements that make up the work week for the new business owner, your "to do" list will always be full and the best you can hope for is to keep it relatively under control. If, in the first several years of business, you have lots of time to sit and watch the tube, either your overhead is too high or you're not making any money. The TV will become specifically functional as either a stress manager or a sedative.

Start working on a business plan now. Earlier I mentioned, as a sophomore in high school, I was on the springboard diving team. One part of practice that still sticks in my head was viewing the movies of the particular dives being done correctly. We would just sit and watch for hours, over and over again. The diving instructor firmly believed in training the mind to "understand" the proper execution even without actually doing it. The business plan presents the same mental opportunity. By spending months on the detailed preparation of the document, you will be able to conjure up an image of each section and quickly recall the strategy at the time of development.

Finally, get some practical experience so that you know what to expect. If you can reduce the amount of unknown territory that you have to cover, the more comfortable and quickly you can do it. On the outside, you can't afford to spend eight weeks learning a skill that you could have acquired part-time when you were "gainfully employed." Be a sponge. Learn all you can before you jump.

These examples are clearly not all-encompassing. However, they will help focus your thinking as you decide what it will take to prepare for the challenge, mentally. Some will think that I have made a bigger deal than necessary on preparing yourself health-wise for the road that lies ahead. With all of the preparation that I did, at this writing, I can honestly say that I have never been so tired. And it is a different kind of fatigue. It is a drained numbness. Every day you learn the ability to power-up to whatever challenge you face. Clients and friends will see you as upbeat and energetic. But, just below the surface, with minimal effort, you could slide off into a hotel and sleep for a month.

The other obvious reason for health consciousness is the simple fact that if you don't lead the charge every day, no one else will. Initially, you are the only one with your best interest at heart. Others may be unwilling or simply unable to fill your shoes. On this front, I believe that you can't be too covered by insurance.

The opening paragraphs of this chapter described my college experience, but it didn't tell the whole story. It didn't mention the fainting spells, or the occasional numbness in my legs, or the stress-related upset stomachs. In this particular case, I had probably crossed the line of good judgment. I am reminded of a line in a famous Clint Eastwood movie where he said, "A man's gotta know his limitations." My college days allowed me the opportunity to look those limitations right in the eye. Again, I call this "knowing the edge." I would argue that a more thorough understanding of your "edge" is in order if you wish to prepare for what you will encounter.

If a certain athletic shoe company were writing this section, they would no doubt conclude with a phrase like, "Just get tough."

Lesson #26

Physical and mental "fitness" is one of the most important factors in initial business success. No one is willing to follow a leader who cannot lead on a daily basis. Having your own company is just too hard to not be at the peak of your game.

Chapter Twenty-Seven

Cultivated Cavalry

"You miss 100% of the shots you don't take."

– Wayne Gretzky

Sun Tzu was a Chinese General in the year 500 B.C. He was the first person credited with documenting issues of war in his famous text, "The Art of War." These include such topics as "Waging War, Offensive Strategy, Terrain, etc." So pervasive were his insights that his principles still form the foundation of all Asian military strategy and are taught in military schools around the world.

My firm belief that all business strategy is grounded in military history led me to revisit this text when I was just beginning the business planning process. When I left high school in 1974, I had a congressional nomination to West Point. For a variety of reasons, I didn't go. But this does give you some indication of my interest in the topic. I went back and reread a lot of this literature for the express purpose of using it as a basis for my business's strategic planning. Much of the final document was a direct result of this material.

In the book, "The Art of War," in chapter VII, titled, "Maneuver," there are two principles that serve as the focus of this section; numbers 11 and 18. Principle #11 says this, "Those who do not use local guides are unable to obtain the advantage of the ground." Number 18, while a little more obscure, says the following, "Now gongs and drums, banners and flags are used to focus the attention of the troops. When the troops can be thus united, the brave cannot advance alone, nor can the cowardly withdraw. This is the art of employing a host."

145

I have never been a big networker. Yet, I know people who love to drop names like snowflakes when describing who they have had lunch with last, presented to, or just met at a party. While these are clearly helpful contacts in terms of breaking the initial ice, the superficialness does little good when the least bit of doubt is raised by a third party. The difference between business contacts and allies is virtually day and night. So the next time someone tells you they have a contact for you, be cautious in approaching that person because they may not be close at all.

It was our second week in business, and I was lining up our first real round of presentations. The business plan, sitting on the corner of my desk, reminded me that company credibility was something we were going to have to earn over time, and that we were in a very weak position out of the chute. The initial job then, was reestablishing and fortifying relationships with people who knew me already and whose confidence I had gained over many years in the business. While I had a lot of "contacts," what I needed to get the ball rolling were people who had either worked with me in the past or who had very close confidants who did.

My first call was to an old agency buddy who had moved on to greener financial pastures at a different shop in town. He had also managed to jump up a rung on the management ladder, which put him in a much different decision-making bracket. While I realized he did not have the final power of approval to hire my company, I knew that if I could convince him of the quality of the service and its potential value, I would have a key "host," or inside salesperson, to shepherd my efforts and guide me through the maze of internal politics.

Scheduling the presentation was no problem. I managed to get in quickly to see him and an important counterpart. The day of the presentation, I was at a peak and things seemed to click along as smoothly as possible. The enthusiasm shown during the follow-up question-and-answer period would tempt the novice into believing that things would move along quickly. But experience had taught me that this was going to be a much tougher sell up the chain of command than met the eye. With my flag firmly planted, I pulled into a mall parking lot to write up my meeting notes while they were still fresh in my mind.

Time passed, slowly. We had several follow-up meetings and lunches to discuss the possibilities. In my heart, I knew that he was doing his best to find the right opportunity to use me, but was having a difficult time selling it. Struggling to be patient, with my bank account on the decline, and 14 months after our initial meeting, the phone rang with the approval of our first contract. We crunched a month-long project into two weeks, literally working day and night. I had intentionally priced it so that it would get approved, so our profit margin was very small. But it didn't matter, we were in the door.

If there is one thing that I practice religiously, it is following up on completed projects. It is our standing policy to send out evaluation forms with the finished job that allow the client to measure our work in a variety of areas. These are all returned to me personally, for review and action as necessary. Having received an excellent evaluation on the job, I waited about two weeks and called to see how the final internal presentation went. Beaming with joy, my buddy proceeded to expound on the details of a major win for he and his staff with their clients. He couldn't say enough good things, and while I struggled to contain my excitement, it took two days to come down from the ceiling.

As an aside to this story, these folks have since become the best client we have, accounting for a majority of our initial billing. Our service has even been recommended to the agency's President of North America in New York. And to think it all started with a couple of lines on a scratch pad.

What is the point here? It may seem painfully obvious to some that you would employ the assistance of a trusted friend when trying to get started. However, what is not so obvious is the risk the inside person takes in working hard and going out on a limb to help you. They have more to lose than you will ever imagine. How would you ever explain to your boss why you fought so hard to get a particular vendor an assignment if, once you did, they blew it and made you and your company look bad? By being the vendor who chokes, you have not only killed your future chances for business, you have severely damaged the career of a friend. And remember, your buddy has a family and house payments that are a lot more precious than you are.

The point is, you are only going to get one good shot. You must make the protection of your inside contact the number-one priority in your life if you wish to succeed long-term. When they are in doubt, reassure them. When they have a problem, solve it. And when they need it tomorrow instead of Friday as planned, get it to them, no matter what. Don't take a chance with this relationship. Nurture it. Cultivate it. And above all, make them the hero.

Trust me when I tell you, someday you will need – not want, but need – to make a sale. There will be very few people in this world you can turn to. When the accountants are circling your financial wagons, it will be nice to know that you can call the cavalry, the cultivated cavalry.

Lesson #27

Selling your products and services has two levels at the client, internal and external. You can be responsible for the external sales presentation and persuasion process. However, when you are gone, the internal selling begins. You must identify and cultivate the ongoing assistance of these internal supporters.

Chapter Twenty-Eight

The Big Pitch

"There ain't no rules around here!
We're trying to accomplish something!"

– Thomas Alva Edison

One of the best things that I ever did, both in writing this book and in starting my own business, was to tell others that I was doing so. By throwing my intentions on the table, I was compelled to show progress and go through with it, or face the dire humiliation of being labeled a loser. But the real key for me was to cut off any "escape routes" when things got tough. This was it, no changes or tag backs.

I had a buddy reading selected chapters of this book as it was coming together. He is a professional writer in his own right, so I very much valued his comments. At lunch one day, while musing about one of my latest efforts, he looked me straight in the eye and said, "So where is the silver lining?" Stunned a bit by his bluntness, I stammered for a response to his seemingly straightforward question. "Whadda ya mean?" was all I could come up with. For the next several minutes, he proceeded to tell me that this entrepreneurial story sounded too much like a pain in the ass and suggested that people wouldn't buy it if it didn't have a happy ending. So, have you made a million bucks? Are you famous? Are you the talk of the town? Are you seen at only the finest social gatherings? In short, what is the payoff for enduring all of this grief you have laid out so far?

The ride home was an introspective one to say the least. My company was less that 18 months old. I was "working" 20 hours a day. Every dollar that came in was used to upgrade our systems and response capabilities. Credibility was building, slowly, as expected. We had made it through our first year with a net profit. But we were far from out of the woods by any means. My wife and I hadn't been to a social gathering for nearly a year and a half. My golf clubs had been used twice in two years. So where was the silver lining so far? Thus, this chapter.

It took three trips to the car that early, crisp morning to bring all of the presentation material into the conference room for the meeting. With the flip of a switch, the overhead projector jumped to life. I remember the smell of the cinnamon rolls on the table with three pots of coffee that sit on those hot plate warmers. Sipping the morning's second cup, I proceeded to set up the chart stands and unpack the 177 transparencies for the presentation. This was going to be a three-hour marathon, and would prove to be the catalyst for any additional business from this client. To say it was important would be a major understatement. As my nerves began to twitch, I recalled a former boss's philosophy on stage fright, "No one is going to die today," he was famous for saying. With a deep breath, and a few attire adjustments, I was ready.

The first few attendees were relatively junior level people who might have come as much for the doughnuts as to hear my presentation. Chairs at the large oval conference room table began to fill. I had expected an audience of 10, there would be nearly 30 when I started. There was all of the pre-meeting handshaking and pleasantries that one would expect. And while I was introduced to each person on their arrival, admittedly, I would be hard-pressed to recall 20% of their names. My mind was staunchly focused on the, material in the presentation.

My host client gave me a glowing introduction, and then, as they say in the business, it's show time. As I walked to the front of the room, I distinctly remember being struck by a sense of destiny. Instead of being nervous, a great calm came over me, to suggest everything was going to be all right. The room full of alert faces only served to focus my purpose. I had trained my whole life, in many indescribable forms, to be there at that moment in time. And it felt wonderful.

Words began to flow as if scripted. All of the tools I had built for myself were at my disposal. And for three hours, I would conduct the symphony I had practiced for so long. Folks, it is one thing to hear the music, but it is quite another to lead the band. On this particular day, I learned the addictive feeling of mastering my trade. I had done many presentations for my old company, in their style and under their banner. But this one was mine, to either win or lose. And on this day, my company and I were winners, and I was hooked.

Only my watch served as a tangible reminder of how long I was up there. The light applause and kind words after the meeting served to reinforce my feeling of bliss. With the room now empty, I collapsed in a corner chair feeling much like a rock star after a big show. I was completely spent. It took me an hour to pack what had taken only 20 minutes to set up.

The project had taken seven days to build. Two weeks later, I received a check for $9,000. Now most people at this point will be doing the math. I can just hear it now, "You mean to tell me that you can make nearly thirty six thousand dollars a month?" That's what a calculator tells me.

So, the silver lining is the big money? No, one of the upsides is the possibility of doing well financially, and your sudden realization that it is, in fact, possible. Most people who work on salary or for an hourly rate, both of which I have done, can hardly imagine the possibility of that much money, more or less the actuality. On this day, I was convinced it could be done.

But the money was only a small part of the equation. Ninety percent of the silver lining for me was experiencing the power of winning and what it feels like, if only for a fleeting instant, to be the champ. It will grab you and shake you to the very foundation of your soul. It is a feeling that is as addictive as any drug and twice as euphoric. It will haunt you and take you to places you never dreamed possible. It is that which solidifies your resolve.

In another section, I stated that I believed that most people start their own businesses for reasons other than money. Clearly, entrepreneurs are not philanthropists. However, for me the silver lining has become the desire to win, according to my definition, and knowing what it feels like to do so. No matter what challenge you decide to take on, there will emerge a clear definition of what it means to win and lose. Successful companies are obsessed with winning. It sculpts everything from your corporate image to your investment in the future. If you are lucky enough to be bitten by the success bug early in your new business, I would suggest that you are well on your way toward building a successful company.

When was the last time in your life you truly felt like a winner? Your big pitch is just waiting to happen.

Lesson #28

The reward for starting your own business, and the reason you continue despite the many challenges, is the addictive feeling you get when you "win," regardless of how you define it. Another benefit is the realization that financial independence is a very REAL possibility.

Chapter Twenty-Nine

Trial by Patience

"The future is much like the present, only longer."

– Don Quisenberry

The low-pitched buzzing of my computer is the only sound that breaks the surrounding darkness of my office. It's 10:32 p.m. on a Wednesday evening, and once again I find myself alone. As a child, I was afraid of the dark. But now, I find tranquility in the desensitized silence. Only now can the day's activities be replayed and analyzed, and milked for the learning. It is also a time of reconfirming goals and kindling the motivation to keep going. I have learned to use it as a time to regain control of things that can be controlled, and releasing those that can't.

In writing this section, I seriously considered summarizing all of the clichés in the process of attaining long-term goals. You know the ones I mean, like, "Rome wasn't built in a day." I also thought about analogies of things with ageless reliability, like London's "Big Ben." I even groped around for references to sports figures whose years of training allowed them to win the big game. But somehow, all of these things fell short of my purpose in raising the subject of Patience as it relates to my entrepreneurial journey. Perhaps the real reason is that its critical importance and intangibility has rendered me unable to clearly articulate the core essence of its role.

Any casual observer will tell you that it takes sacrifice to firmly plant a new business. Of course, this is true. And the sacrificing takes many forms. For a person like myself, who has left a successful career complete with all the salary, benefits and travel perks, the start of a new small company

153

is like trying to kick a drug habit. In all the senses of the word, one can easily become addicted to an environment whereby the flimsiest of reasons will quickly result in plane tickets to Los Angeles and a three-night stay at a four-star hotel. The corporate "hook" can be deeply set and sometimes self-inflicted.

Regrouping from this addiction brings into focus the interrelated issues of "patience" and "sacrifice," perhaps even making them one in the same. Maybe my earlier inarticulation can be captured in the phrase, "The patience to continue sacrificing." This is the challenge you all will face.

Before I left the ad agency, my wife and I were a particularly well-traveled couple. We would take two and sometimes three expensive vacations per year, most of which included sun, sand and sea. There were few things materialistically that we went wanting for. My job afforded me the opportunity to travel nearly whenever and wherever I desired. In short, it was like having someone else pick up the check on a dream date. This is not to suggest that it all came without a price tag, because it definitely did. But it is important to remember that this game was being played with funny money.

All that stopped when I made the long walk to the parking lot that fateful Friday afternoon. For those leaving the corporate world, look forward to the same. The "detoxification period" has been long and challenging. The most difficult challenge has been to listen to friends and acquaintances discuss jetting off to LA for this and that, or introducing you to their new vehicles and wardrobe. Very few "unnecessary" things have been purchased in the last two years. All of our time, effort and money has gone back into building the business. A friend of mine in Iowa said to me a month before I opened my business, "Well, if you're going to make it, you won't be playing much golf or buying anything expensive for a while." Truer words have never been spoken.

But what does all this have to do with the "patience to continue sacrificing"? If you have started your own business or are seriously contemplating it, you are most likely a person who can establish and attain long-term goals. That may well be the easy part. What I am referring to is the pressure, real or imagined, to digress and begin thinking with your heart instead of your head. This distraction may cost you more than you can imagine.

It is important to remember also that the whole notion of sacrificing encompasses more than just material objects. Self importance and ego are indulgences that will have to be reduced, if not eliminated. Confidence is something that will continually be attacked, but cannot afford to be relinquished. Credibility will have to be rebuilt with painstaking care. You will find it has been sacrificed in the career change.

The point to all of this discussion is that, while it is all right and sometimes necessary to splurge and "let off some steam," mental discipline, combined with objective focus, is the only way you will survive both the short-term "withdrawals" and the need for sacrifice. It is almost like staring your challenge in the eye and seeing which one of you will blink first. Don't let down your guard under any circumstance or pretext. Each day must be thought of as a single piece of a much larger puzzle under construction, if you have any chance of making it. Further, in my view, it is critical to create the environment whereby you feel you have learned or gained something new from each differing experience. This perspective empowers you in a situation where you can easily feel overwhelmed.

"Rome wasn't built in a day." There, I said it. I'm sorry, but it is true. You must give yourself the flexibility of time, without becoming a procrastinator. Move forward whenever you can, but realize that things will take time. One of the biggest sources of frustration for me is what I must sacrifice for my family, and not just myself. No more big, expensive vacations. No new cars on the horizon. And my wife's list of "special things" had to go into the drawer.

But as I sit here banging away at the computer keyboard, as mentioned in the previous chapter, I am staunchly convinced of the "potential" and my ever-increasing ability to achieve it. Folks, the brass ring is out there, and I have seen it. Now, with each new grab, the effort becomes more calculated and refined. Don't allow the frustration of impatience to hinder the clarity of the focused effort.

In the immortal words of Bill Murray in Caddy Shack, "Be the ball."

Lesson #29

Great companies are built one stone at a time. You must develop the patience and determination to craft your dream and realize that time is an ally.

Chapter Thirty

Chasing the Horizon

*"The average man, who does not know what to do
with his life, wants another one which will last forever."*

– Anatole France

In October of our first full year, weak with exhaustion and
bordering on depression, my wife and I concluded that a
vacation was the only answer. Scraping together the money
necessary to run to Florida and hide in our secret spot, we
nested for seven days as the rain established our agenda for
us. We were sick and lethargic. So much so, in fact, that it
was the first vacation I ever recommended coming home
from early. With all the challenges that had been faced in
the months leading up to this getaway, it was clear that we
were a couple who was in desperate need of some good
news.

On the way to dinner one night, in a driving beach-type
rainstorm, we happened to pass a local fortune teller. The
office was right on the main drag, in a good part of town,
seemed clean and inviting, so with nothing better to do, we
decided to give it a try. The woman who greeted us was
obviously Indian- as in Far Eastern- in her early 40s with
long jet black hair. She seemed pretty normal in her dress
and mannerisms, in other words no cheap parlor gags. My
wife was first in for a visit, returning in about 20 minutes,
for exactly $20. I was next.

With a slight squint of her eyes, and a poker straight face,
she began to tell me things about myself that I was shocked
to think about. The accuracy of her words cut me like few
things before. At the end, she said that I could ask her one
question, as long as it wasn't about money. Without so

much as a hesitation, I inquired about the future of my business. She said that I would be successful in a business where I helped other people achieve their goals. But, this success would come only after many obstacles had been overcome.

I left her office having gladly parted with my $20, with the first good news I had heard in a long time. At the time, I was sure it was divine insight. (Remember, I was in search of good news.) But in retrospect, it was a simple statement of fact that anyone who was in business, and she obviously was, could have predicted.

This episode did two things for me. First, it forced me to reexamine all that had happened so far from a slightly different perspective. Maybe before I had been too "hopeful" that I would be successful, and not determined enough. Second, it taught me that control of my destiny was not necessarily divine, as much as it was up to me to get off my butt and go accomplish it. Isn't it funny that when people talk about something "being in the cards," it is generally when something bad happens. Positive outcomes, conversely, we love to take credit for as some form of skill or cunning. In short, losers talk about predestination, winners talk about accomplishment.

When I got back from Florida, I had a whole new attitude. It was now time to attack and analyze, then repeat, repeat and repeat. No more wishing. Just attacking. Many motivationalists refer to this in their presentations. Often, the analogy is between planned and unplanned attempts at goal attainment. My purpose in bringing it up to you here is that time passes much too quickly to wish that things will happen. The only time things do happen is when you make them happen.

I have a buddy who went on a special golf weekend with me last year. On the drive up north, we got on the subject of goal attainment. In one of those "late at night go ahead and be blunt" attitudes, I asked him point blank what his goals were for the rest of his life. There was an uncomfortably long pause. Then come the somewhat distressed look and the soft, "I'm not sure," response. My friend is not alone. Millions of people, from all walks of life, not only don't have a plan in their lives, they don't even have a destination. When the same question was shot back at me from my buddy in the car that night, I had a list of things as long as your arm. I tried to put it into perspective for him by saying that given the challenge of writing my own epitaph, I would want it to consist of specific accomplishment and not just personality characteristics.

"Why?" was his retort. "Who are you trying to impress?" This was an excellent question, and one that I had not considered to the extent of being able to quickly formulate an answer. But it was at that moment that it dawned on me. I'm the one I'm trying to impress. I have become addicted to taking on formidable challenges and beating the odds. And not just the easy ones. In springboard diving, they have what is called "degree of difficulty." The harder the dive is to perform, the greater the multiplication factor against your score. In a nutshell, while you may look good for the judges and the crowd, few contestants ever won a diving meet by doing all easy dives. It was clearly the hard ones that separated the cream from the milk.

Now in my life, I have chosen to stop doing all easy dives. I would much rather take on a challenge that was formidably difficult and fail than to have coasted smoothly without a scratch. On a ski trip some years back, a friend crystallized this point for me. After boasting on the last day that I had gone the whole weekend without falling, he turned to me and said, "And you're the worst skier of the four of us because you're afraid to ski the tough hills and learn new things." And he was right.

In choosing the underlying theme of this book, I did not make a hasty decision in a flip moment of foolishness. Over many weeks of searching my heart about how to convey to readers the innermost reasons for starting my own company, it became obvious that my very outlook on life had changed. Learning to "chasing the entrepreneurial horizon" is about not taking life as it comes, but rather taking life by the throat. Believe me, others will not understand your incessant goal setting and accomplishment cycles. But with every degree of elevation comes a clearer view of the vista that more timid souls only dream about.

Yet, how high is high? Only you will know the answer to that. If you really chased the horizon, obviously you would never catch it. But if you chased it long enough, in the pursuit you would have circumnavigated the globe, taking in all the wonders along the way. Eventually, you would return to the same point at which you started. Those who did not choose to go would chide you for such a hard and foolish venture only to return to the same place. And in the end, we all stand in the same place anyway, one person who chased and one who did not. Now I ask you, which would you prefer to be?

Lesson #30

Life is not a dress rehearsal. Through every experience, good and bad, there is a learning and insight that transcends the process of attaining it. "Sailing to new lands inherently demands that you lose your fear of not seeing the shore."
Author Unknown

Chapter Thirty-One

A Thought for You

"Don't tell people how to do things. Tell them what to do and let them surprise you with their results."

– George S. Patton

When you decide to embark on the entrepreneurial journey, you will encounter few sign posts. There are a great many service companies out there that will teach you the mechanics of having your own business. Some of these are outstanding and recommended. In this book, I have toiled to present the emotional side of the undertaking in the most sincere and timely fashion I know how. My reasons for doing so are not altogether altruistic. Some are very personal.

This country was founded on the basis of the entrepreneurial spirit. America's allure globally is the proposition of opportunity and reward for diligence and sacrifice. We are truly in trouble as a nation if this ideal is snuffed out. It symbolizes the core value of what it means to be an American. Yet, it is still the path less traveled and not for everyone.

I believe that people develop codes of conduct by which they live. Sometimes these are learned, modeled, or forced upon us, but we all have them. The judgment of this code is the basis of much that separates us as people and as societies. I've come to have my own code as well, that serves as a template for me to hold close when making very personal decisions. I'm not talking about religion, per se, but rather about personal philosophy.

We have come a long way together in this book. I want to leave you with my adopted personal code or philosophy. Maybe it will inspire, comfort, motivate, guide and light your way to the successes you seek as it has for me.

Lesson #31

Regardless of what happens, always remember that you have to look at yourself in the mirror each and every morning. Do what is right in your heart and you will never fall victim to regret.

If   **by Rudyard Kipling**

If you can keep your head when all about you
Are losing theirs and blaming it on you;
If you can trust yourself when all men doubt you,
But make allowance for their doubting too;
If you can wait and not be tired by waiting,
Or being lied about, don't deal in lies,
Or, being hated, don't give way to hating,
And yet don't look too good, nor talk too wise;

If you can dream-and not make dreams your master
If you can think-and not make thoughts your aim;
If you can meet with triumph and disaster
And treat those two impostors just the same;
If you can bear to hear the truth you've spoken
Twisted by knaves to make a trap for fools,
Or watch the things you gave your life to, broken,
And stoop and build 'em up with worn-out tools;

If you can make one heap of all your winnings
And risk is on one turn of pitch-and-toss,
And lose, and start again at your beginnings
And never breathe a word about your loss;
If you can force your heart and nerve and sinew
To serve your turn long after they are gone,
And so hold on when there is nothing in you
Except the Will which says to them: "Hold on;"

If you can talk with crowds and keep your virtue,
Or walk with kings-nor lose the common touch;
If neither foes nor loving friends can hurt you;
If all men count with you, but none too much;
If you can fill the unforgiving minute
With sixty-seconds' worth of distance run-
Yours is the Earth and everything that's in it,
And – which is more – you'll be a Man, my son!

About the Author

Throughout his life, Steven H. Brown has always enjoyed a challenge – even if he had to create it himself – compiling an enviable résumé in a wide range of endeavors. Steve earned a congressional nomination to West Point, supervised truckers at UPS, bulldozed his way to an MBA from Michigan State University in record time, and successfully climbed the corporate ladder at advertising-agency behemoth DMB&B only to gamble his future on a dream. Like the Energizer bunny, he just "keeps going and going..." And succeeding.

For his latest accomplishments – or to leave a message – please visit www.shbrown.com.

CPSIA information can be obtained
at www.ICGtesting.com
Printed in the USA
BVHW011314270919
559633BV00010B/66/P